JEALOUS

How the scandalous love of God invites us near.

*A six-session Bible study
on the Book of Hosea*

Rebekah Johnson

WESTBOW
PRESS®
A DIVISION OF THOMAS NELSON
& ZONDERVAN

Cover designed by David Livingston

Unless otherwise indicated, all scripture quotations are from the English Standard Version Study Bible (Crossway, 2008).

WestBow Press books may be ordered through booksellers or by contacting:

WestBow Press
A Division of Thomas Nelson & Zondervan
1663 Liberty Drive
Bloomington, IN 47403
www.westbowpress.com
1 (866) 928-1240

ISBN: 978-1-5127-8639-2 (sc)
ISBN: 978-1-5127-8638-5 (e)

Library of Congress Control Number: 2017907616

Print information available on the last page.

WestBow Press rev. date: 08/11/2017

Plant the good seeds of righteousness, and you will harvest a crop of love.
Plow up the hard ground of your hearts, for now is the time to seek the Lord,
that he may come and shower righteousness upon you.

—Hosea 10:12

CONTENTS

INTRODUCTION

Thank you for committing to study the book of Hosea. Prepare to be surprised, quieted, and comforted by the jealous love of our God. Prepare to read some passages that make your face hot with conviction, while tears of healing possibly fall in the next chapter. Some verses will silence you because of the holiness of God, and others will pull you forward in your seat, eagerly looking for Jesus's fulfillment of this scripture. Prepare to discover the power of the gospel packed deep into this Old Testament prophet.

Prepare to read more than a lighthearted love story. This is much more than a story of a generic, feel-good love that swoops in and saves a woman with poor self-esteem. While it could appear to be that at first glance, we will be studying for much more.

If we do not, then a few months from now or a few heartaches later, our comfort may be only inches deep and our self-worth merely propped up, rather than reaching deep. If we approach Hosea primarily to tend to our feelings and self-esteem, then we will miss the deep freedom and joy that is ushered in when we discover truth.

Would you study deeper with me? Could we look hard at this book, with our minds going ahead of our hearts?[1] Could we, together, look closely at each character and each interaction? Could we learn what was going on in Hosea's world some 755 years before Christ—the Christ who makes this love story relevant to us?

This study is not formatted like most Bible studies on the shelves today. At the beginning of each week, you will find five days of study. The questions will take you through the scriptures, engaging first your mind and then your heart and your hands. After the five days of study, there will be a brief narrative of my applications and my affections that have been stirred from the scripture. In this portion, I hope to color in what I have learned from this Old Testament prophet, as I share some of my stories of grace.

Prepare for a very rewarding six-week study that pulls together the historical perspective of young Israel and the fulfillment of Jesus's work on the cross. I hope all of these elements, as well as my honest confessions and stories, will encourage you as you move through the book of Hosea. Hosea's messages are words breathed by our husband-God and are intended to leave us in awe.

Let's get started!

THE GIFT OF A HUSBAND-GOD

HOSEA 1

DAY 1

Read Hosea 1.

Why was this book written, according to Hosea 1:2?

The book of Hosea is about God's love and faithfulness toward his people. However, you must understand that God is first and foremost faithful to himself and to his covenant. Read the following verses that describe aspects of God's covenant with his people. What did God require of his people, and what did he promise his people, according to the following verses?

Genesis 12:1–3

Exodus 19:5–6

Let's also take time to understand what life was like in Israel at this time. Turn to the following verses and match them with the description of Israel at the time of Hosea's ministry. These verses will paint the backdrop of Hosea's experience as he preached to God's people.

2 Kings 14:23–25	There were many evil kings over Israel, in a short amount of time, due to assassinations.
2 Kings 15:19–20	Jeroboam II was king in Israel and did what was evil in the sight of the Lord, just like his father.
2 Kings 15:8, 14	Israel made a deal with Assyria but then secretly made a deal with Egypt. When Assyria discovered this, they besiege Samaria, the capital of Israel.
2 Kings 17:3–5	Assyria was paid off by a weak king of Israel to bribe him not to attack the capital, Samaria.
2 Kings 17:7–16	A summary of Israel's behavior and why God punished them.

From the very beginning of this study, we see that Israel's behavior contrasted greatly with what God had asked of them. Who they had become varied greatly with who God intended them to be. Each chapter will describe the many aspects of Israel's unfaithfulness toward the God who loved them as well as God's responses to them.

DAY 2

Read Hosea 1, again.

From Hosea 1:2, what does God ask Hosea to do?

God gives Hosea this unusual assignment *before* he gave him the message to preach to Israel and Judah. Why do you think God did this?

Let's define the metaphor introduced in chapter 1, verse 2. Hosea represents God, and Gomer represents Israel (and us). We will unpack this metaphor throughout the study, but at first glance, in what ways do you think of God as your husband?

Does this concept comfort you or make you uncomfortable? Why?

Read Isaiah 54:5–7. Rewrite it in your own words in the space below.

DAY 3

In Hosea 1:3–9, you read that Gomer has three children, and Hosea gives each a name that describes the consequences of being unfaithful. You will see these names throughout the study.

First, Gomer conceives and has a son. What do they name him?

What does that name mean? (Use a dictionary, if needed.)

The Valley of Jezreel was within Canaan—the Promised Land for God's people. Jezreel was a great battlefield, and in Israel's history, it was a place of victory. Record what happened in the following scriptures at Jezreel:

Judges 6:33

Judges 7:19–25

Yet after Israel strayed from God, there was a different kind of battle at Jezreel. In 2 Kings 9–10, there is a civil battle because of idol worship among God's people. Jehu, the Israelite, attacked Joram, the king of Israel, to punish him for his Baal worship. Some commentators state that although Jehu obeyed God's command to kill the family who brought Baal worship into Israel, Jehu was also arrogant and reckless. He surpassed God's desire for justice and behaved like a madman; he was brash and impetuous, creating a mess.[2]

Is there an area of your life that was once defined by victory and honored God but now has become a mess of a place because of sin?

Too often in my life, when I behave like I am god, I hurt a lot of people and leave a mess in my path. Have you ever noticed that when you make yourself a god, you create a disaster? Explain.

In Hosea 1:6, Gomer has a daughter. What do they name her, and what is the meaning of her name?

In Hosea 1:8, Gomer has a third child. What is his name and the meaning of it?

At times in my life when I felt alone or abandoned (like *Not My People*) or starved for mercy (like *No Mercy*), it was good for me to see that those feelings were brought on by my own unfaithfulness. Have you ever experienced this?

DAY 4

The names of Hosea's children give us our first look at the effects of disobedience in this book. Thankfully, God's jealous love is such that it cannot sit idly by why his people are unfaithful. Look up the following verses and note what you learn about God's jealousy.

Exodus 34:12–14

Ezekiel 39:25

Look up the word *jealousy* in a dictionary and write the definition that best fits with what you think the Bible teaches about God's jealousy.

How could God's jealousy be a good thing for us?

Throughout Hosea, we will learn that God's jealous love prompts him to act on our behalf, and for his own glory. Unlike Hosea, we have the privilege of spanning out to grasp God's big story, which includes Jesus and the gift of grace. Turn to the following New Testament verses and note how they connect with the names of Gomer's children.

Romans 9:23–26

1 Peter 2:9–10

What goodness is ahead for Israel and Judah after their season of judgment? Rewrite (paraphrase) Hosea 1:10–11.

The "yet" in verse 10 is our gospel hope in the first chapter of Hosea! Although God's people were not behaving like God's chosen people, God would remain faithful to his covenant. Throughout the pages of Hosea, we will see the hope of the gospel and that what we deserve contrasts greatly with what we receive. While our infidelity should bring us death, we continue to receive the love of a faithful husband-God.

DAY 5

Read Hosea 1 again, drawing together all the details we have looked at this week.

In contrast to the warnings made apparent by the names of Gomer's children, turn to Micah 6:8 to learn the positive imperative of what God requires of us.

Look closely. Can you see how these three requirements parallel the three names of Gomer's children?

In every situation in life, we have an invitation to respond in faithfulness or unfaithfulness. In what ways could you seek justice instead of disregard it? In what ways could you welcome more mercy into your life? In what ways could you walk closely with your husband-God, rather than live with distance?

Spend some time thanking God for his jealousy that is intolerant of competition. Thank him for his grace that beckons us near to him, time and time again.

THE GIFT OF A HUSBAND-GOD

When the first week of a Bible study has you studying words like *Jezreel* and wants you to identify what disasters you are leaving in your wake, you may be wondering why you put this book in your cart. And trust me: I was there too.

It is a bit heavy.

And by "bit," I mean it's super, crazy heavy.

But here is our hope when it feels that way. Consider this image: God's covenant love for his people is like a solitaire diamond ring symbolizing faithful love and everlasting covenant. That love is our hope as we study Hosea. Our sin and the ways that we are unfaithful to God are like the black velvet placed behind the ring, making the diamond shine brilliantly. Each week we will see that our frail and capricious affections for God can serve as the black velvet behind the treasure of the gospel. Our husband-God's love contrasts greatly to our own. Like a diamond of unmerited love, God's love for us shines all the brighter against the darkness of our sin.

Because of this, let's bravely study this book in its entirety, including the heavy days. We will travel through some tough sections of the Old Testament to better understand Hosea's audience in Israel, but we will also hop over to some comforting stories in the New Testament. In the Old Testament, we will read about God's holiness and Israel's sin. In the New Testament, we will read about Jesus and how he abolished condemnation for those who trust in him. As we focus our gaze on this love, like a new bride staring at the ring on her hand, we will find the will and the grace to turn away from empty love and disastrous sins.

The book of Hosea is, indeed, a love story written over a span of thirty years. Hosea's job was to be the mouthpiece of God, relaying messages to God's people. Hosea's audience was primarily Israel, from 755 to 720 BC, beginning when Jeroboam II was king.

The book begins as Hosea is given a unique assignment from God. The Lord said to Hosea, "Marry an unfaithful woman and have a family. And in this way, you will better understand what I am experiencing as my people give themselves away to Baal." Hosea would soon learn that this firsthand experience would add so much more empathy and strength to his sermons.[3]

Hosea obeys and marries a woman named Gomer—a woman of adultery. She was likely a prostitute before her marriage to Hosea and returned to that lifestyle after her marriage.[4] This analogy in chapter 1 begins to paint the picture of how God loves the seemingly unlovable.

Gomer symbolizes Israel—the faithless yet loved bride of God. While in a covenant with God and living within the land God had given them, their hearts were still far from God. During this time, the people of God were looking a lot more like their Canaanite neighbors than the children of a holy God. They had alliances with pagan countries and shared their gods and religious practices. As we saw in 2 Kings, God's people were disobedient to the law and practiced idol worship. They trusted in the comforts and strengths of neighboring countries rather than trusting in God and his covenant.

Hosea symbolizes God, teaching us that God desires us to see him as husband. By designing this metaphor, God invites us to ponder, *Who am I as husband?* John Piper captures it perfectly when he invites us to "love God warmly as husband, rather than serve him dutifully as master."[5] Before we address how God handles the unfaithfulness of Israel, we should fully consider this view of God.

It is at this invitation that we must slow our study, briefly. We must pause and recall that this story, primarily, is not about us. Before we can uncover truths about ourselves, we should gaze on the truths about God. While we will learn much about our own hearts in this book, the main character of this book (and every book in the Bible) is not us but God.[6]

God is portrayed as a husband who desires intimacy with his bride. His love is so pure and jealous that it must be intolerant of any competitor.[7] There is no question that this metaphor can warm our affections. Perhaps it brings images of a young husband anticipating his wife walking down the aisle or of a devoted husband of seventy years still holding hands with his first love. But for many women, this analogy could fall short. Maybe divorces or broken relationships have fractured your image of a good husband. Maybe you are fighting an uphill battle in your own marriage or feel stuck in your singleness. The invitation to think of God as your intimate husband may fall short or may repulse you completely.

For where this analogy works for you and for where it does not, we can exhale into the embrace of our husband-God. Even the most attentive and forgiving husband in the room cannot compare with our God as husband. There is no human love that can forgive as completely, reconcile so fully, and love so extravagantly. For every aspect that left you lacking by human love, our husband-God can fill with his faithfulness, justice, and mercy. He is a benevolent God who loves us with an everlasting love. Jeremiah 31:3 declares, "The Lord appeared to us in the past, saying: 'I have loved you with an everlasting love; I have drawn you with loving kindness.'"

It is after we set our eyes on our husband-God, who is the main character of this book, that we begin to understand who we are.

If I'm being honest, on most read-throughs of Hosea, I want to resonate more with the prophet than with the harlot wife. I suppose I wish the lessons to take from this are from Hosea's example, not Gomer's. My mind's eye pictures us, sitting around hot cups of coffee, discussing how to be brave mouthpieces for God—how to simply obey and speak his messages with courage. I can just picture it: I would read the verses of Hosea and you would nod with me, saying, "Yes, we *must* tell all the wayward children of God that his love cannot stomach competition."

I wish that was the lesson from this Bible study. I wish my position in this study was from behind the pulpit or beside righteous Hosea.

However, a few months into this study, I saw myself more accurately. While my self-righteousness would convince me otherwise, I am certainly not the forgiving husband. And I am not simply a member of the audience to Hosea's messages, nodding in agreement. I am not on a stage with a microphone warning "lesser" women of their disobedience.

No, I have fallen from the pulpit and landed at the brothel.

I am unquestionably the adulteress wife. I am the woman in a marriage covenant with God, enjoying living with his promises; yet in so many ways, my heart is far from him. I am the woman bent on chasing lesser lovers. I chase after quick satisfaction, pleasures that my eyes can see, and comforts to prop up my ego.

I am the woman who has it all wrong about my husband-God. I have kept him at a safe distance, like that of a master. A distance where I don't have my weaknesses revealed, where I think my messes are hidden. I have resisted his advances and filled in the space with other lovers. His desire for me makes me uncomfortable, so I fill in the space with idols that are a lot less soul searching. I stiff-arm my husband-God and his desires for a pure love and instead entertain the gods of this world: comfort, wealth, and security.

In this study, I must accept that I am the loose woman to the same degree as Gomer and Israel. My infidelity has been found, and I deserve nothing less than the names of Gomer's children. I am deserving of the name *Jezreel* as my apostasy has produced disaster. I am the destructive woman capable of massacres. Like Jehu, in my prideful days of unfaithfulness, I am capable of hurting so many people. When power entices me and I chase a secure future full of control, I become consumed with selfish ambition. In 2 Kings 9, the watchmen recognized Jehu because he was riding like a madman. I can imagine my children viewing me much the same. "Mom is home, and she's coming like a madman!" (That would be funny, if it weren't so true.) When I surpass God's heart for justice and instead behave like I'm the queen, my tongue is reckless, my moods are volatile, and my reactions are abusive. When pride and idolatry go unchecked in my heart, I am a disaster waiting to happen. These days of unfaithfulness sow for me God's discipline, just like Israel.

Because I have cheated on the covenant love of my husband, I am deserving of the names *Lo-ruhama* and *Lo-ammi*. My self-love invites his mercy to be removed from me and my relationship with him to be cut off. My offenses toward God are so vast that what they produce should leave me as an orphan starved for mercy. My unfaithfulness has earned me nothing less than divorce.

Would you sit in this uncomfortable place with me? Could we let this confession linger long enough that we begin to squirm? Could we bravely consider that just like Israel, what we are is far from what we were intended to be? Could we truly believe that we belong on the stand of the courtroom? Could we stick with this study long enough to find out our verdict?

While this book and this study have yet to fill us with warm fuzzies, ensuring us that we are as loveable as we had hoped, could we bravely continue? Although this book does not give us quick pick-me-ups or pad our identity, could we read for much more? Could we dig in to discover the heart of the God who created us for intimate relationship with himself? The heart of the God who tells us his story of redemption from Genesis to Revelation. This book is packed with all the hope, comfort, and love that we desire, but not until we first see the truth about both God and ourselves can we grasp it.

Could we see the ways that we are the metaphorical woman in another man's bed? Do we see that we are the untrue wife of God, sneaking away from him or drunken at an orgy for Baal? Do we see the areas of our heart that are filled to overflowing with corrupt pleasures, celebrating the gods of this world rather than our husband? And can we see it, even if we have kept it hidden in the discreet corners of our hearts?

Until we sit here, in this dark day of honest soul searching, we cannot move on in the book of Hosea. If we still think we are on Hosea's team, more like God than like the harlot wife, then we will miss the freeing gift that is beautifully wrapped in this book: the gift of a God who would rather love like a husband than rule like a master.[8]

He is a God who sees us, understands us, and loves us before we love him.

He is a God who married a faithless bride, with eyes wide open. Knowing she would soon be bent on lesser lovers, he entered a covenant with her. Knowing that she would soon forget him and spend her beauty on the gods of her neighbors, he extended his love. He is a God who is overflowing with forgiveness and second chances, a God with a big-picture plan to make grace the way to relationship. The gift of a God who is more than master, his love is like that of a husband, longing for nearness and intimacy.

As an amazing grace weaves through the pages of Hosea, we will see that what we receive contrasts greatly with what we deserve. Unlike Hosea's original audience, our study of Hosea will include the perspective of the New Testament. In each chapter, we will consider how different our situation is now because of Jesus. If we are in Christ, then the days of study that are heavy with condemnation will be lifted by recalling the gospel. When in a relationship with Christ, what we receive is grace instead of death. While we will see that this does not exclude us from times of discipline or experiencing the painful consequences of rebellion, we can rest knowing that Jesus took our ultimate punishment on the cross.

As we study this book of warning, could we also hear the comforting invitation extended to all of us? Contrasting the consequences of unfaithfulness, Micah 6:8 invites us to do justice, love mercy, and walk humbly with our God. When we are given a job from God, we should humbly accept it and obey. However, there is a temptation to pridefully boast of it and carry out an adulterated version of God's work, as Jehu did at Jezreel. As we enjoy the mercy of God through Jesus, we should delight in showing it to others. And rather than holding off God at a safe distance, we are invited to let him near and walk humbly with him in relationship. While unrepentance in our hearts tells us to stiff-arm our husband-God, grace invites us to come close and link arms with him, like a young bride enamored with her husband. The fruits of faithfulness are, indeed, far better than what our unfaithfulness sows.

The invitation to repentance and faithfulness are laid out for us in this first chapter. The invitation to step into the light (albeit an unflattering light) allows us to see that we are sisters of

Gomer. And while that is a major theme of this book, God's word will not leave us condemned and rejected. This book is about a jealous love of a husband-God. We are greatly loved by a great God. In this book, we will see the worst views of ourselves. Yet it will be repaired by the mercy of God, his faithfulness to a covenant, and the promise of Jesus. There is a heavenly love that tolerates no rival from our husband-God. Let's fix our gaze on him and watch as his jealous love invites us to come near and remain there.

BROTHELS OF THE HEART

HOSEA 2:1–12

DAY 1

Begin by reading all of Hosea 2.

According to 2:2, what is the charge brought against Gomer?

According to 2:3, what is the penalty for this offense?

Ezekiel 16 is a parallel scripture with Hosea and is an allegory describing God's faithless bride. List all that God does for his bride from Ezekiel 16:6–14.

How did his bride respond to him in Ezekiel 16:15?

From Ezekiel 16:59–63, what is the good news for the Lord's faithless bride?

How is that good news for you?

DAY 2

Gomer is charged with unfaithfulness and committing adultery. Recall that she is symbolic of Israel. Referencing 1 Kings 16:31 and 22:53, who is Israel's other lover?

Using a dictionary, can you find what kind of god Baal (translated "owner" or "master") was?

Consider for this moment: are you guilty of similar charges as Gomer and Israel are? Who are your other lovers?

According to Hosea 2:5, how are Gomer's other lovers paying her for her acts of prostitution?

How would you differentiate bread and water, wool and flax, and oil and drink? What are the varying purposes of these pairs?

Who do you credit for the provision of your daily necessities like bread and water?

Do you trust your own strengths and gifts to cover your shame, like how clothing covers our nakedness and shame?

Are there false gods or idols that you credit for your gifts and luxuries?

DAY 3

Look ahead to Hosea 2:8. Who gave Gomer her grain, wine, oil, silver, and gold?

Gomer (and Israel) was confused about who gave her what she needed and wanted for "the good life." How did this misunderstanding hurt her marriage?

Consider the following verses. What material needs are provided for us? By whom?

Luke 12:22–28

Consider the following verses. What immaterial needs are provided for us? By whom?

Luke 11:13

Isaiah 61:10

How should knowing these truths affect our relationship with God?

Write out one of your favorite "God stories" of when God provided a big need for you (material or immaterial).

DAY 4

In Hosea 2:6–14, there are three *therefore*s.[9] As you look briefly at them, what should we learn about God by looking at this repetitive phrase?

We are going to look closely at each of these. The first *therefore* is in verse 6. Using the ESV translation, look at verses 5 and 6 to fill in the blanks below.

Because   Gomer   _____,   God   will
_____ so that she cannot _____
_____.

Find the following verses, and write them out below.

Job 1:10

Lamentations 3:7

Have you ever sensed that God has blocked a path that would lead you away from him?

Have you ever seen God slow you from your runaway path from him?

Because of this rescue plan, what goes seemingly wrong for Gomer in Hosea 2:7?

What decision does Gomer make in Hosea 2:7b?

Turn to Luke 15:11–24, and note what similarities you see in these two stories.

Tim Keller, in his book *The Prodigal God*, defines prodigal as "recklessly spendthrift, to spend until you have nothing left."[10] Based on that definition, who is the true prodigal in this story? (Look carefully!)

How is the dad similar to how God is portrayed in the book of Hosea?

How has your husband-God been recklessly extravagant with you? (We will see this again in Hosea 3.)

DAY 5

The second *therefore* is found in 2:9. Staring in verse 2:8, fill in the blanks below.

Because Gomer didn't know _____, and because she used those gifts for _____, God will _____ _____.

What did Gomer and Israel do with the provisions God had given them, according to Hosea 2:8b and 2:13? Turn to Ezekiel 16:17–19 to further explain this thought.

Often, my temptation is to keep God's gifts and provisions for myself, to increase my comfort and feelings of security, rather than give them back to God in worship. Is there a gift or possession God gave to you that you give to your other lovers, rather than give back to God?

Spend some time thanking God for the gifts that came to your mind, and ask him how you could give them back to him.

From Hosea 2:9–10, what does God remove?

God has removed Gomer's wool and flax, which were used to cover her nakedness. Turn to Genesis 3:6–7 where Adam and Eve became aware of their nakedness. What did they use to cover themselves?

In so many subtle ways, I pridefully say, "I got this covered, God. I don't need you." I then trust in my good deeds and strategies to cover my shame and make me look good. Can you relate with me in this way?

What did God use in Genesis 3:21 to cover Adam's and Eve's nakedness?

What significance is there that God sacrificed an animal to cover their shame?

Have you ever felt exposed? Has there been a situation that left you with your sin, mistakes, and imperfections on display for all to see?

In John 8, there is a woman who was exposed in this way. Read John 8:1–11. What was this woman caught doing? How do you suppose she was dressed in this moment?

Who caught her in her sin, and where did they bring her?

How did her situation end?

Because of Jesus, how did her situation end differently from Israel's in 722 BC? Refer to 2 Kings 17:6–15.

What a hope we have in Jesus! When we trust in him and accept Jesus's blood as our covering for our sins and shame, we do not get the condemnation our sins deserve. What a love from our husband-God! What a grace!

BROTHELS OF THE HEART

The poetic images of chapter 2 are powerful and romantic; they are that of a persistent, purposeful husband. They are of a man on a mission, strategically working to win back his beloved wife from her many other lovers.

His first strategy to repair the broken relationship is brought on by Gomer's confusion. Gomer, or Israel, seems convinced that her lovers have provided her with both her necessities and luxuries needed for "the good life."

Israel is convinced that Baal, the god of her neighbors, has given her what she needs and more. Baal was the god of the Canaanites—the god of the sun and fertility. He was also seen as the god of weather and agriculture. Israel believes that Baal gives life, essentially. Furthermore, she believes that she has earned her riches. So she adamantly purposes, "I will go after my lovers." She sets off, away from the home of covenant love and down the paths leading to the doorsteps of her other lovers. Maybe casually at first and then more adamantly with time, she sets off to brothels of the heart. Places of weak and empty love, places where love is cheap and short-lived.

In an effort to correct Gomer's wrong thinking and bring her near again in covenant love, God blocks her runaway path. His strategy is to frustrate and deter her in the pursuit of her lovers. Can you see her, hurrying down the paths that she has learned well, paths worn down by her nightly routes? But now, there is a hedge in the way. Along the path to her lovers, he has walled up her way so that she cannot find her route. Can your mind's eye picture Gomer parched with thirst, already dry as a desert, navigating paths blocked with thorn bushes? Did she try to push through anyway, until the piercing thorns of warning drew blood, finally deterring her?

We are often confused too. As our hearts, hands, and homes fill up with all we need for "the good life," we forget God. As dreams come true and daily bread becomes the norm, we drift away from truth and near to the lie that *this world* provides us with what we need or that *we* have earned our necessities and luxuries. As it says in Deuteronomy 8:17, "Beware lest you say in your heart, 'My power and the might of my hand have gotten me this wealth.'" Israel did just this, as do we. God's people had received manna bread from heaven to fill their stomachs, water from a rock to quench their thirst, and oil and wine for their pleasure, but they started to believe that they earned these gifts. We drift away from the truth and toward the lies that this world provides us with what we need or that we have earned our necessities and luxuries.

Although I say that Jesus is the giver of life, I often behave as if I believe something quite different. Often my attitudes and reactions reveal that I believe that someone or something else provides my bread and water, my wool and flax, and my oil and wine. Consider this with me: if we credit our paychecks with providing our daily needs, we are at risk of loving our jobs more than our husband-God. This will lead to us putting our trust in them. If we believe that our ability to organize, charm, or work hard provides us with our wool and flax, then those abilities can easily become a false god. In moments where we pridefully say, "I got this covered," are we trusting in a false god, rather than the grace of our God? Are there luxuries in your life that you attribute to your superior health or impressive family rather than seeing them as an extravagant gift from God? When we displace gratitude or trust for these provisions, our relationship with our husband-God is at risk. We are at risk of forgetting God, just like Gomer.

Because of this, we too insist on leaving our husband-God for our other lovers. Gomer declared, "I will go after my lovers," and left the goodness of covenant love. We often are like a passionate yet misguided, teenage girl, running away as we yell to God, "Let me go!" (And what we are running away to is as unimpressive as our junior high crushes: lanky, acne-faced, and pubescent. You are picturing him, aren't you?) We run away from our first love, seeking out our other lovers and the false security that they give us.

Sometimes our departure from God is fast and dramatic, but more often, our heart drifts away slowly and subtly, enticed by the subtle, false promises of lesser gods. Our forgetfulness about our husband-God produces confusion and casually leads us to the doorstep of weak lovers. We set out, maybe sneakily or maybe incidentally. In the metaphorical dark night, we begin to wear down paths to brothels of the heart.

At these brothels, we find an exciting love that we can feel and see, and it is easy to justify. At these brothels, we seek love from this world, and we give ourselves to gods that will not love us back. We exchange covenant love for emotional highs and empty promises. Maybe your other lovers resemble my own—a savings account, a plan for my future, the sense of being in control, and the absence of enemies, distress, or difficulty. I chase after these as if they provide for me what I want and need in life.

Yet because of the jealous love of our husband-God, we find obstacles in our heart's path. To the left there's a wall; to the right the path is blocked. On stubborn days, we rush right past the thorns of caution and feel the sting of them piercing into our flesh. No matter our efforts, we cannot find our lovers.

It is there, when our frustration is high and our energy is depleted, that we hit our knees. It's right there, on the trail leading away from covenant love and near to our idols, that we must give up the chase. Frazzled, grieved, and likely annoyed, we must stop the futile pursuit.

It is in that moment, on that path, we are invited to notice how similar we are to the son in Luke 15. Thinking that our gifts and possessions are rightfully ours, we claim with passion, "I will go! I will go to ensure I get what I desire and what I believe I deserve." Are we not like this son (and Israel) who received an inheritance we did not deserve and gifts we did not work for?

Tim Keller further explains this thought when he says, "Are we not like the younger son, when our behavior says that 'we want our Father's thing, not our Father.'"[11] Our hearts hardened from misplaced gratitude to this world and bent toward lesser loves, we resonate with the younger son. Our feet begin to wear down paths to brothels of the heart, places of reckless passion and empty love. Like the prodigal son, we set our hearts on giving our gifts to the gods of this world, seeking quick pleasure and fictitious security.

Not until our path is hedged up, and we are graciously blocked by God, do we begin to see the reality. Not until mercy slows our runaway path do we pause long enough to once again relearn his love.

Like the son in Luke 15, it is a good thing when our frustration leaves us with the conclusion to return. When our plans for "the good life" go up in smoke, when our expectations dissolve right before us, when our hearts are broken from the abuse of this world, we have a fresh invitation to return. Like the son returned to his father and Gomer to her first husband, our husband-God bids us to come to him.

What amazing grace! What an extravagant grace that allows us to return, after we have been so reckless. Although we have despised God, choosing instead dead gods, false securities, and short-lived pleasures, his grace paves a way home. Our husband-God is the prodigal God, recklessly and extravagantly offering his love and forgiveness to us. Knowing that I still fall short of understanding how good his love is, he allows me to return to him, time after time. Knowing my most secret and subtle idolatry, he continues to meet me on the road home. His love is so excessive and based on his goodness, rather than my own, that my walk of shame is transformed into a walk of atonement. The days near to our husband-God, even if defined by discipline and quiet modesty, are indeed better than our days of seeking pleasures. The road away from home, near to our lesser lovers, paved with misplaced gratitude and idol worship, will lead to only a damaged and abused soul. The road home, near to our prodigal God, will lead to life and freedom.

Can you see this extravagant love at work in your life? God loves you enough to let you experience frustration, in hopes of keeping you near. God is not a killjoy, but he is passionately jealous for your affections. His love is so big that it hems us in. Psalm 139:5 says, "You hem me in, behind and before, and lay your hand upon me." Have you ever noticed God's hand ahead of you, keeping you from running away or going somewhere too quickly? Have you ever sensed his hand behind you, protecting you, and pushing you away from a shameful or hurtful situation? His thoughts are so much higher than our own, and he is able to see what is actually good for us and leads us in that path.

Often, I think our destructive paths are blocked, and we are not aware of it. You likely do not actually sneak out at night to another man's bed or to bow to a hidden gold statue. But consider the last time you felt incredibly frustrated because your plans wouldn't pan out or felt like God was keeping something from you, something that you thought would be a good thing to have. Have you ever had a decision move so slowly that you get discouraged and finally give up, to later realize that it would have put distance between you and God? Have you ever had a goal that you just couldn't overtake, a goal that you would seek but never find? Looking back, could it be that achieving that goal would actually be arriving at an idol?

Let's take the time to unpack the truth about our idols, lest we miss the salvation of identifying them. John Calvin says, "Man's nature, so to speak, is a perpetual factory of idols."[12] Grown-up idols can be tricky. We disguise them, even within the costumes of religion or benevolence. We place them up high on the mantle of our hearts and keep dust bunnies far from them. We care for them like beloved pets or houseplants—feeding and watering the roots of them, allowing them to flourish in our souls.

For those of us in the church, we would never dare have a twelve-foot idol that we bow down to in the middle of the cul-de-sac. But what about twelve one-foot idols concealed within our homes and our hearts? I know that is more my style.

I suppose I convince myself that false gods are easier to control than the Living God. So in hopes of getting the life I can control, I have quietly bent low to restrictive eating, compulsive exercise, precise budgeting, and an etched image of having it all together. These dead idols that I have fashioned myself breed a false security when they are mine and mood swings when I fear I am losing them.

In the subtlest of progressions, I am an idol worshipper. When did life going my way nudge ahead of loving the husband-God that loved me first? When did a life plump with material possessions, positions of comfort, and plenty of surplus lead me away from the true God who loves me like a wife?

These mini-gods that I think about more than my holy God, these selfish goals that I'm convinced will get me where I want to be, only leave me tired, lonely, and very grouchy.

What was your most recent mood swing? (Yes, I'm serious.) It's good to laugh and roll your eyes at yourself but then to zoom in and assess if it was brought on because a false idol didn't deliver like you had preferred. Your bad attitude can be a helpful symptom of idolatry in your life.

Hosea explains that Israel is guilty of the same idolatry. Not only does Israel forget who gave her the grain, wine and oil, and silver and gold, but she gives these gifts to Baal. These goods that she believes she has earned, as payment for her acts of prostitution, she is now setting before Baal as acts of manipulating worship. The provisions from God are now being used in pagan worship.

The second attempt to restore the marriage is like the first, in that it doesn't seem loving. God says he will take back the grain, wine, wool, and flax. Not only will he block her from going to her other lovers, but now he also will allow her to experience need and shameful exposure. He is going to remove the provisions in which she has taken comfort to remind her that they are not from Baal. This Canaanite sun god was getting credit for what her husband-God had given her. Hosea is warning Israel that their unfaithfulness to God is going to bring on judgment, as he has warned them from the very beginning.

God warns them that he is going to take away their crops when they ripen, disarming their belief in Baal as the god of the sun. He would also remove the wool and the flax, which were used to make clothing, intended to cover their nakedness. As we saw in 2 Kings, Israel would soon be encircled, literally, by Assyria. Her crops stolen by her neighbors, her shame would be on display for all her weak lovers.

Within this second attempt, God also allows her to experience shameful exposure, which we see in the very beginning of the Bible in Genesis 3. When Adam and Eve broke the covenant with God, they immediately felt shamefully exposed. When Adam and Eve first felt guilt, they reached for a covering. In a hurried attempt to hide what was bringing them shame, they sewed together fig leaves. Although their early understanding was probably limited, all they could perceive through their shame was that they didn't want the other person seeing them. The immediate reaction was to conceal their brokenness from each other. Alan Kraft's explains it well in *Good News for Those Trying Harder*.

> They (Adam and Eve) hid—not only from God—but from each other. Well aware of their reality, they instinctively tried to make it look like they had it all together—and we've been doing the same thing even since.[13]

Adam's and Eve's leaf coverings were a pathetic attempt to cover up what they had done. But God mercifully provided them with a more sufficient covering. God made the first animal sacrifice and used its skin to cover Adam and Eve. Showing grace, God didn't give them as their sin deserved, but he allowed them to live and provided a covering for their shame.

Is this not an early picture of the Messiah to come thousands of years later? After thousands of years and millions of animals sacrificed, God would provide the ultimate sacrifice of Jesus. He would spill his blood so that we would no longer carry the shame of our sin but wear the robe of righteousness. Isaiah 61:10 says, "I will greatly rejoice in the Lord; my soul shall exult in my God, for he has clothed me with the garments of salvation; he has covered me with the robe of righteousness." When in Christ, we do not get what our sins deserve but are given life.

As we saw in chapter 1, what we receive contrasts greatly with what we deserve. We see that while we are sufficiently covered in Christ's robe of righteousness, Jesus was stripped naked and bore our shame. While our unfaithfulness earns us such guilt and humiliation, it was Jesus who received the heavy hand of discipline. This is our gospel message.

This is where we must keep our eyes fixed. As Hosea pinpoints our sins, our response must not be to just try harder to be pure. We cannot *will* ourselves to clear out the brothels of our hearts in our own strength and strategies. The invitation is to behold Christ, whose sacrifice *allows* us to be the wife of our husband-God. It is God's grace that teaches us to say no to ungodliness (Titus 2:12). Resist the urge to pull yourself up by your bootstraps. (Although I'm sure they are fabulous boots.) Instead, fix your eyes on Jesus and rejoice in your salvation. Join with the psalmist when he says, "But I have trusted in your steadfast love; my heart shall rejoice in your salvation" (Psalm 13:5).

The account in John 8 of the woman caught in adultery helps us understand and even accept times of shame. Like this woman in John 8, the law finds us in the bed of the world. As Paul explains, "Through the law comes knowledge of sin" (Romans 3:20). Just as the Pharisees (the so-called keepers of the law) found her in her sin, God's perfect law exposes us in our trespasses. When our unfaithfulness is brought to light, we must not try to squirm free of the accusations. Though this is incredibly uncomfortable, it is pure grace to be found out. As our face burns hot with shame and our guilt tries to swallow us whole, we nevertheless must choose to embrace these opportunities for genuine repentance. God's invitation to us is to let his Spirit use the law to bring to our attention all the ways that we cheat on our husband-God. Then we must allow him to draw us out, away from our sin. We can do this in confidence because God's grace will not leave us naked and surrounded by accusers but safely at the feet of Jesus. Like this woman, because of grace, we receive new starts, not stones. Again, Paul speaks to this when he says, "Now the law came in to increase the trespass, but where sin increased, grace abounded all the more" (Romans 5:20). When we resist these opportunities to come before Jesus—exposed, naked, and ashamed—we are shorting ourselves of his abounding grace. Although we deserve the judgment described in Ezekiel and Hosea, we are instead granted a gracious reset. When we are in Christ, mercy—not condemnation—is what we are awarded. Jesus responded to her, "Neither do I condemn you; go, and from now on sin no more" (John 8:11).

I had a season in my life a few years ago that left me found out and face down in the sand at Jesus's feet. (You will hear me reference this season of discipline throughout the study.) My husband and I worked in youth ministry at a large church. After several fruitful years, pride subtly snuck into our hearts and made a home. I began to believe that my abilities were providing my daily needs, that my talents were giving me the luxuries that I loved. I bowed to the idol of people pleasing and began thinking I deserved for everyone to like me. In the subtlest of ways, I was my own god—building my own queendom behind the veneer of God's work.

God graciously allowed me to be found out. Over the course of a few months, a couple of people who had been hurt by my pride put words to what was going on in my heart. They came to me at different times, hurt and angry, and called me out on my pride, selfishness, and manipulation. The conversations were pretty void of mercy, and I have learned to be thankful for that because, just like the woman in John 8, I needed to be yanked out of the bed my sin had made. I needed their resentment and hurt to encircle me, causing heat to rise in my face, guilt to threaten my heart, and fear to shake me. This season of being found out did not bring condemnation.

Although my accusers were right, they were not allowed the last word. Although the law was highlighting a long list of offenses on my account, what came next was not exposed nakedness or wrath.

There, in the most unflattering light, grace abounded all the more. When my trespasses were many and oh-so-ugly, grace became an ocean. Possibly the greatest miracle of my life, I experienced God ruling victoriously over my flesh and inviting me to lean into his discipline. While squirming out of their accusations could have brought some momentary relief, the long-term consequences would have been less grace in my life.

From the middle of a circle of criticism and shame, I looked up and beheld the face of Jesus. He asked me to feel the weight of my sin, to own my ability to be untrue. But after repentance, he pushed a reset button. Because of grace, the law brought me near to Jesus. I stayed there for a while, on my knees (in some ways on my face), in a season of discipline. There were months, even years, of spiritual recovery ahead. But Jesus's words in my ear drowned out all others. "Neither do I condemn you; therefore, go and from now on sin no more" (John 8:11).

Can we be brave women who lean into seasons of being found out? Could we fill our churches and our women's ministries with a courage that trusts our husband-God's jealous love? He loves us too much to let us sleep around with all the lesser loves in this world. So when the law comes and yanks you away from your other lovers and securities and quick fixes, bravely allow it! Although it's painful and it's scary at times, sit tight and let the process bring you to the feet of mercy. When you feel like your sin and regrets are brought to light, lift your eyes to Jesus, and by the power of the grace in his eyes, turn away from your sin.

WEEK 3

A DOOR OF HOPE

HOSEA 2:13-23

DAY 1

Begin by reading all of chapter 2, again.

Last week we saw Israel's confusion about who gave her her necessities, comforts, and pleasures. We also read that she took those gifts and laid them at the altar of Baal, in idol worship. We read how God rescued her from her mistakes, both by blocking her paths that led away from his love and allowing her to experience want and shame. Now we will read about another rescue mission from her husband-God.

The third *therefore* is in 2:14. Referring to 2:13 in the ESV, fill in the blanks below.

Because Gomer _____ and _____ herself, and went after her lovers and _____ the Lord, God will _____.

Do you notice a change in tone in verses 14–23? How would you describe it?

Look up the definition of *allure* and write it below.

Gomer is allured away from the celebrations of Baal by her husband. Where does he lead her?

31

Refer to Exodus 13:18. Where did God bring the Israelites when he rescued them from Egypt?

Can a season in the wilderness (literally a desert) be a good experience? Explain.

From Hosea 2:14, how does God speak to Israel?

"Speak tenderly to her" in Hebrew literally translates "speaks to her heart." Write out Isaiah 40:2 below.

Read Romans 2:4. What leads us to repentance?

Is there a time in your life that you have experienced this kindness of God? Describe how God dealt tenderly with you and how that led you to repent.

Recall a time that God allured you out into a desert. Can you see how God spoke tenderly to you there? Can you discern why the time in the desert was needed?

DAY 2

From Hosea 2:15, what two things does God do for his bride in the wilderness?

Read Joshua 7, and note what happened at the Valley of Achor.

What type of a first was this for Israel, since being led into the Promised Land?

In what ways was Hosea's audience behaving like Achan?

Use a dictionary to find the definition of the word *achor*.

When someone recalls my biggest mistakes, I naturally feel a lot of fear and shame. What might some of the original audience have felt when they remembered what trouble occurred at Achor and how it related to their own behavior toward God?

What does God change their trouble into, according to verse 15?

Read Acts 28:20. What does Paul call Jesus?

Consider an area of trouble that you need Jesus to turn into a door of hope.

A DEEPER LOOK

WHEN GOD IS NOT ENOUGH

Turn to Joshua, and read chapters 6 and 7.

What well-known battle do we read about in chapter 6?

What was God's instruction in 6:18?

Specifically, what did Achan take from the Canaanites in 7:21?

What was the sequence of events of Achan's sin? (Look closely at 7:21.)

    1.

    2.

    3.

Where did he hide the treasures?

In what ways did his behavior say, "God is not enough"?

Let's contrast him with a Canaanite woman from just a few chapters earlier. Read Joshua 2.

What was Rahab's job?

What did she know about the God of the Hebrews?

In what ways did she say, "God is enough"?

Achan was an Israelite man who had just experienced the goodness and power of God in the battle of Jericho. Yet with rubble still falling and thick dust still in the air, his heart went hard and amnestic. Although God's people had been instructed not to take any plunder from the battle, Achan saw some items of beauty. While God was enough to defeat Jericho, God was not enough for him in the moment following. He would need *just a bit* more. So he smuggled some Canaanite gold, silver, and clothing and hid them within his tent, buried below the surface.

In a quick moment of doubt, he doubted God's sufficiency. He decided that he also needed items to make him feel secure. Have you ever been there?

Achan's sin wasn't covered up for long. God revealed his sin, and his destruction was within the same day. The place of his unfaithfulness was named Achor, meaning "trouble."

Are we any different from Achan? Do we not love our God of victory? But in so many secret ways, do we not say, "God is not enough"? Has God not flattened Jericho for us, time and time again? But when we see the devoted things of our neighbors, we believe we might need *just a bit more* than God. So we smuggle them near. We hide them, in our homes and just below the surfaces of our heart. Of course we believe that God is good, but we *also* believe that we need a bit more: the golden reputation, sterling riches, even the nice clothes, the savings account, the income, and the solid gold approval of women. These are the items that we hold close, telling ourselves that we are more secure because of them.

We convince ourselves that if our forbidden treasures are out of sight—hidden below the surface and tucked behind the walls of our homes—then they will not be a problem.

So we hide them behind our front doors, just like Achan, never to be brought out in public. We smuggle in our secret addictions and weak loves, our doubts and our idols, and store them below the surface of our hearts.

But our cover-up will not last. And while they may not be revealed today, they are a cancer hiding in our hearts. The items of destruction that we shamefully love are caustic to our hearts, our families, and our churches. The riches of this world that we hold close, as a way of supplementing God's power and love, will lead to our ruin.

Could we be like Rahab instead? Could we live a life that says, "God is enough"? No matter our circumstances, our bad habits, or our shame, could we leap out in faith? Could we leave the securities of what we know—the tall and thick walls that we live in—and be freed from their capricious security? Rahab didn't know that much about God. She just knew that he was a God who freed his people. And that is all she needed to know. She believed that freedom could be hers—freedom from her past and freedom from shallow love.

Unlike Achan, she believed that God was enough. She didn't have to supplement his power with any comforts. She didn't wait until he proved himself and provided her with a plush life. She believed in what she could not yet see (Hebrews 11:1).

The life lived in faith, trusting that God is enough, will far exceed a life lived in unbelief. Unbelief prompts us to take control and smuggle the things of this world near, to fabricate a sense of security.

Faith prompts us to trust in the sufficiency of God's love. Faith asks us to bravely uncover what is right below the surface of our hearts. It asks us to bring into light the items of destruction that we keep close so that our husband-God can change these troubles into hope.

Today, could you open up to the Lord and to a friend or family member about what you have tried to keep hidden? Is there an area of shame that needs to brought out so that it can point you to the hope of Jesus? Is there guilt or bitterness that is slowly eating you from the inside out? Trust in your husband-God enough to confess it, and watch as he leads you to the hope of the gospel.

DAY 3

What change do we see in how Gomer answers her husband in Hosea 2:15–16?

1. She answers him as she did _____.

2. She will now call him _____ not _____.

Married couples often watch their wedding videos on their anniversaries and find refreshment from recalling their young love. Turn to Exodus 15:1–18 to see how young Israel rejoiced in God's love.

The people of Israel often overlapped their worship of God with Baal, to such a degree that some thought they were the same deity. In Hosea 2:16–17, God clears up the confusion. Why do you think that it matters that Israel addresses her husband-God differently at this point?

From chapter 2, recall the meaning of the name *Baal*.

Read Luke 15:11–32, again but take notice of the older son.

From Luke 15:28, what was his reaction?

Did he join in the celebration?

Who came out to meet him?

From Luke 15:29, in what ways did the older son seem to view his prodigal dad as master?

I am much like the older brother, viewing God as my boss that I want to impress. I wrongfully think of my good acts and obedience as chips to stack up and someday cash in, saying to God, "You owe me this or that." In this way, I am actually making myself god, hoping to manipulate and control God.[14]

There is much at risk when we view our God as a master, rather than a husband. At this point in the study, how would you say you view God?

DAY 4

Hosea 2:19 says, "And I will betroth you to me forever. I will betroth you to me in righteousness and justice, in steadfast love and in mercy." Look up the definition of *betroth* and write it below.

Betroth:

In Hosea's time, an engagement always included a bride price.[15] From verse 19, what payment is made?

According to verse 19, of whose righteousness and justice is he speaking? Whose steadfast love, and whose mercy?

Our relationship with God is only possible because of *God's* righteousness, justice, love, and mercy. Read Romans 5:8 to recall that our relationship with our husband-God begins before we have earned his favor.

Hosea 2:20 says, "And you shall know the Lord." The original translation of *to know* is the Hebrew word *yada*, which refers to a husband knowing his wife intimately. We will see this word throughout the book of Hosea. Turn to the following passages in the ESV to better understand the meaning of the original translation of *to know*. (You might need to look at your footnotes.)

Genesis 4:1

Luke 1:34

How would your relationship with God look differently if you knew him with a *yada* knowing, rather than merely a head knowledge?

DAY 5

Read Hosea 2:21–23, again.

These remaining verses in chapter 2 give us a sneak peek at the very end of the story—speaking of the day of Christ when God's relationship with his people is no longer affected by sin and the real God of the sun and weather rules.[16]

Recall Gomer's children from chapter 1. Note how each name changes once we are fully rescued and redeemed.

Jezreel:

Lo-ruhama:

Lo-ammi:

What is the difference between "God scatters" and "God sows"?

Take a few moments to pray a prayer of thanksgiving. Thank God for his patience and kindness that leads us to turn from sin and false gods, each and every day. Thank God for creating a covenant that allows us to be his loved children that he plants for his good pleasure.

A DOOR OF HOPE

The Lord's next attempt to repair his covenant marriage with faithless Israel is much easier to read. After blocking her path and frustrating her attempts to run away, he then lets her experience want and shame. But in the second half of chapter 2, we find a soothing change of tone. It is here that Hosea describes God's third strategy to bring Israel back to him.

Israel invited discipline by participating in the feast days of Baal while dressed in typical prostitute attire. Adorned with rings and jewelry, with makeup and facial tattoos, Israel would participate in these feasts, engage in orgies, and burn sacrifices to the pagan god of the sun and fertility. The feast days were very erotic; prostituting oneself was seen as worship to Baal.

Therefore, God allures her into the desert. He romantically entices her *away* from the feast days of Baal and *into* the wilderness so that he can speak tenderly to her. About what does he speak to her? If we look at the following verses, we will see the answers.

There, in the wilderness, away from the distraction of perverted love, when he has her alone and focused, he gives her vineyards. He nourishes her soul and restores the vines that he previously allowed to be removed. And he speaks of her trouble. He speaks of Achor.

God takes his children back to the memory of Achor, where his people first cheated on him in the Promised Land. It was at Achor that an Israelite man named Achan stole plunder from Canaan. It was here that Israel loved the beautiful but forbidden things of Canaan. And because of this scandalous love, the Israelites were defeated in battle.

Yet as the memory of remorse and guilt was mentioned, God opens up something new. There, in the wilderness, God explains that he will "make the Valley of Achor a door of hope" (Hosea 2:15). There, in the dark valley, where they recall how long they have chosen to disobey, God would make an entrance for hope. Because of the kindness of God, their troubled hearts would find access to hope.

Is this not how God treats us? Does he not see us dolled up to attract the attention of the world? We casually leave him to celebrate the things the world celebrates and to feast on what the world offers us. Rather than celebrating the great love he has for us, we seek the entertainment and pleasures of our neighbors. We make new definitions of what is moral and good according to what they do and forget about the marriage covenant.

But rather than forgetting us or leaving us in the days of discipline, he allures us out into a sacred desert. Away from a corrupt understanding of love, he romantically entices us near to him. Now away from competition and distraction, he renews his love for us. Like a young couple away on their honeymoon, there is now opportunity to be alone.

When we find ourselves there, do we recall how God invited Israel out into the desert? Away from the slavery of Egypt and toward the Promised Land, he led Israel out into the desert. There, God spoke tenderly to his people, leading them with fire and smoke. There in that desert, God provided bread and meat from the sky and sweet water from a rock. He drew her out and away so that she would become his. He enticed her, speaking to her heart, speaking with kindness and promise. And in those early days in the desert, he defined what it means to be in covenant. He gave them the law to say, "These are the expectations of you in this relationship." He also described to his people how he will behave.

By faith, we should see our deserts as holy ground. We will be blessed if we do not resist the invitation to the wilderness. Although these seasons can feel scary and unknown, they are, indeed, rich. What may look like dry desert is most assuredly an opportunity for refreshment. When we allow his love to draw us out, even if to a wilderness, we can anticipate the great kindness of our husband-God to meet us there. When you find yourself there, tune your heart's ear to be spoken to by your God. He will speak to you about himself, about who he is, and what you have been missing about him. And he will speak to you about hope—your hope-filled future.

Our husband-God may also remind us of our days of Achor. As he tenderly speaks to our heart, he may gently bring us back to the days our unfaithfulness began—the early days of idolatry, when we first doubted that his covenant love was enough for us. Like Achan, when we have barely begun to experience the vast goodness of God, we decide that we also need what this world can offer. Like Achan, there in that sanctified desert, we go after the luxuries from which God said to abstain. My eyes see the devoted things of this world: the bigger homes, the name-brand clothes, and the padded savings account. I let them into my eyes and make a home for them in the secret caverns of my heart (Matthew 6:22–23). Like Achan, I dig up a little space for them, hiding them and convincing myself that these loves are concealed and, therefore, not a problem. I believe that as long as the idols are a secret, they will not be an issue.

The Valley of Achor is the very place that we choose lust over covenant love. It is where you and I desire the things of deceiving beauty. When we are reminded of past sin and shame, we are not to doubt God's forgiveness; these times are opportunities to consider if there are still hints of sin remaining in our hearts. Old sins die hard, at least in my life. My sins of ten years ago have a way of morphing to remain undetected in my life. The Valley of Achor is an opportunity to consider what has remained in our hearts.

Yet because of the jealous love of our husband-God, as our other loves are uncovered and punishment is deserved, we discover a gateway to hope. We will no longer find condemnation and death but hope and life because of Jesus. Where severe discipline is warranted, we instead find a passageway to newness. Because of the mercy of God, our dark valleys become avenues of grace.

As you reflect on your Valley of Achor, could you trust in the grace of God enough to uncover what is right below the surface? What sin do you conceal below the surface or behind your front door? Is there a bad attitude, bitterness, or insecurity that you think you can manage, as long as it stays hidden? Our jealous husband-God sees our hearts. While we can hide a lot from the people in our lives, we are kidding ourselves when we try to deceive God. Bring into light what has been hidden in the dark. Daniel 2:22 says of God that "he reveals deep and hidden things; he knows what is in the darkness, and the light dwells with him." Let's fill our homes and our churches with women who regularly and quickly uncover the sins that we would rather keep buried. Let's bravely trust in the love of our jealous God.

At the risk of oversimplifying, let's consider the purpose of doors. Doors are shut to keep things out: bugs, cold air, and sometimes children. Doors are closed to make a separation with something. What do you need to shut the door on, from your past? What idolatry or unfaithfulness do you need to close out? Slam that door of hope in the face of your past shame. (Do it with some attitude!)

Doors also open into newness. They lead us into new areas with different capacities and purposes. Hope beckons us away from our valleys and through doors leading to newness. In what ways do you need newness? Specifically, where does shame need to be dealt with so that hope can create a fresh start? Walk through this door with confidence, believing in the love that is working to rescue and redeem your heart.

How loved we are by God! It is, indeed, quite a kindness that leads us to repentance (Romans 2:4). It is a kindness incomparable that bids us to come near to him, as grace renews our love for him. The grace of God, displayed in Jesus, is a door that allows the unlovely wife to find relationship with God, again and again. Is there a Valley of Achor that you need to believe can be transformed by grace? Is there an area of shame or weakness, a bad habit, that you believe is too offensive for your husband-God to forgive? Could you ponder how high and how deep is the love of God? He doesn't merely forgive when we confess our unfaithfulness; he redeems every valley. As Isaiah 40:4 says, "Every valley shall be lifted up, and every mountain and hill be made low; the uneven ground shall become level, and the rough places a plain."

Gomer's response to this desert retreat with her husband-God is clarity. She now sees God for who he is and Baal for who he is. She will no longer call her husband-God "master." She is no longer making God fit into the boxes that suit her, but she can now distinguish between the true God and the false god. Furthermore, she will answer him like a husband, not a master. John Piper articulates this well when he says that unlike Baal, our God wants to be loved warmly like a husband, not served dutifully like a master.[17] Israel's love is refreshed, like in the days of her youth, like Israel in the days she left Egypt.

Viewing God as a master has dismal consequences, as we saw in Luke 15. The older brother viewed his father like a master to be served dutifully. Yet for many of us, when we read Luke 15 about the prodigal son, we understand (even commiserate) the temper tantrum of the older son. Tim Keller explains it so well in his book *Prodigal God*.

> The elder brothers of the world desperately need to see themselves in this mirror. Jesus aimed this parable primarily at the Pharisees, to show them who they were and urge them to change. As we said, the younger brother knew he was alienated from the father, but the elder brother did not. That's why the elder brother's lostness is so dangerous.[18]

Our entitlement, brought on by viewing God as a master (or even coworker), keeps us on the outside of the celebration. What joy and feasting we miss out on because we would rather work for God's goodness rather than take the free gift of his love and riches.

But when we come near to our Prodigal God, as the messy, indebted runaways that we are, we are greeted on the way home. When our pride is abolished and our false idols have been torn down, there is a great party thrown in our honor. (And there is nothing worse than missing out on a party!) It's an engagement party of sorts, as we are again betrothed to our husband-God. And the power of his proposal to us is that it is based on God's righteousness, justice, steadfast love, and mercy—these gifts serving as the bride price. We are proposed to, long before we have proven ourselves. As we saw earlier, the lover of our souls bases this covenant on his character, not ours. Even when we are faithless, he is faithful (2 Timothy 2:13).

Hosea then spoke of a day yet to come. Promises not to be fulfilled in his time or even a time in the New Testament but a day that is coming, when Christ will redeem all things. Sin will no longer keep us at a distance, and the world will no longer be under the curse of sin. The real God of the sun and the weather will bring all the earth in subject to him. Like a farmer scattering seed, he will sow his people in the land, planting them in love and mercy, as children of God. Like a gardener that plants flower seeds for his pleasure, our God will lovingly plant us in the land.

God's appeal to us is the same as it was to Israel. May we love him with authenticity and candor. His petition, through Hosea, is for us accept his jealous love and to allow him to get as close as a husband. No longer should we think of him like a boss, hoping to impress him, while keeping him at a professional distance. The love of our husband-God is not based on our impressiveness but on his covenant love. Exhale deeply and rest in this freeing truth!

INVITED NEAR

HOSEA 3

DAY 1

Read all of chapter 3.

What good news did we read at the end of chapter 2?

What does the Lord command Hosea to do in verse 1?

What has Gomer done, again?

Who initiates this attempt at reconciliation?

DAY 2

Gomer has returned to prostitution, just as Israel continued to turn away from God. From verse 1, what does Israel love?

How do raisin cakes sound to you? Gross and unimpressive, right? What ridiculous indulgence do you turn to rather than the extravagant love of your husband-God?

Raisins are also an aphrodisiac meant to arouse desire. As you have seen, Baal was the god of fertility and prostituting yourself before him was seen as worship. Why do you think the Israelites turned to raisin cakes?

What do you turn to so that you can feel love? (Could it be as silly as a romantic comedy on Netflix?)

What do you turn to so that you can feel lovely? (Mine is as sad as vacuum lines in my carpet and a spotless sink.)

In what way could these habits lead you away from God?

What do you know about God that could help you turn toward him rather than toward these examples?

DAY 3

What does Hosea have to do in verse 2?

Why do you think he had to do this?

Look up the following verses to understand how we, as the estranged wife, are brought near again to our husband-God.

1 Corinthians 6:19–20

Acts 20:28

1 Peter 1:18–19

Look up the following definitions to add to your understanding of what Hosea did for Gomer:

ransom

redeem

Gomer has made herself a slave, behaving like a captive rather than a wife. Are there ways that we do this? Consider John 8:34.

DAY 4

From Hosea 3:2, what does Hosea pay for Gomer?

Why do you think he doesn't pay it all in cash? (No stressing allowed; it's okay to make a guess!)

Read Numbers 5:11–31, and note what you learn about this barley offering, which is called the "grain offering for jealousy."

What is the accusation against this woman?

What does the husband bring "on her behalf" (Numbers 5:15)?

What is the penalty if she is guilty of unfaithfulness?

In detail, what does the accused woman have to drink?

This is hard to read as a woman, isn't it? Why do you think God's law was so severe?

Turn to James 4:5, and write it out below.

Are you guilty of unfaithfulness? In what *specific* ways have you driven your husband-God to holy jealousy?

Joyfully turn to Galatians 3:13, and write it out below.

Rewrite Galatians 3:13 in your own words.

DAY 5

In Hosea 3:3, Hosea says to her, "You must dwell as mine for many days. You shall not play the whore, or belong to another man; so will I also be to you." Here we see Hosea explaining the game plan for Gomer to learn what life as a beloved wife, rather than a slave, will look like. He is also stating the expectations for their relationship.

Compare that to Deuteronomy 21:10–13, which explains how a captive woman could become an Israelite. List all that this woman has to do to leave her status as a slave so that she may come into a marriage covenant as an Israelite wife.

The word for *covenant* comes from a Hebrew root *karath,* which means "to cut." From what does the woman in Deuteronomy 21:12–13 have to make a cut?

What does Gomer have to cut ways with to be in covenant love with her husband-God?

Just like Hosea removed the other lovers from Gomer, what does God take away from the children of Israel in verse 4? List them below.

Read the following verses to learn why God had to remove their leadership, religion, and false gods.

- Judges 8:22–27

- 1 Kings 16:31

- 1 Samuel 13:5–14

What was the result of removing these things, according to Hosea 3:5?

What needs to be removed or cut from your life so that you may live in nearness to God?

Spend some time thanking God for his scandalous love. His love that pursues the unlovely is shocking and unfit for a holy God, yet we are brought near because of it. Thank him for helping you cut your ties with your past lovers so that you might be in covenant nearness with him.

INVITED NEAR

The upbeat ending of chapter 2 comes to a screeching halt as chapter 3 begins. Chapter 2 ends with Gomer responding well to God's loving rescue of her. She has had a season of clarity in which she no longer is confusing God with Baal. God has renewed his promises to her, promises of a love founded in his righteousness and justice, love, and mercy.

But it seems that Gomer's love has failed again. Beginning in chapter 3, God repeats his command from chapter 1. He tells Hosea to do what he has already done—love a woman of harlotry. Go and love Gomer again, who is loved by another man.

As Hosea's audience watched Gomer leave and receive the love of other men, did they assume the metaphor would end? Did they assume Gomer would now be punished and Hosea freed from his fractured relationship?

But did they hope it would be another way? Did they watch and hope that Hosea would go again and rescue his lover from her defiant choices?

Why does God instruct Hosea to do this? Because God loved Israel, still. Once again, Israel had turned to other gods, namely Baal, and all that was included with the worship of this pagan god, but his love remained.

God comments that the Israelites loved cakes of raisins. John Piper paraphrases this by saying, "They loved Hostess Twinkies."[19] There was likely nothing spectacular about cakes of raisins, except that raisins were an aphrodisiac, which would fit with the sexuality of Baal worship.

It is good for us to see the ridiculous loves of our hearts too. It is a good day when we see that our weak loves are often as weak and sorry as raisin cakes or Twinkies. Perhaps it is a love story on Netflix that we sneak away to, to be engulfed by, or even a level of cleanliness in our homes. To God, who offers us such a satisfying love, these pursuits are as pathetic as raisin cakes.

At times, it's vanity and vacuum lines that I think make me feel lovely. Often I chase after a more ideal figure or a more organized home, hoping to fabricate some feeling of being loveable and acceptable. As I do this, I am bowing down to false gods. I cannot turn to these things without turning away from my husband-God.

As women, we *love* love, and we love to feel loved. So when God's love is hard to feel, there is a temptation to turn away from him and pursue a love that we can feel, touch, and see.

Could it be that our hearts need to be rescued from *raisin cakes?* I believe so. (Because raisins are disgusting anyway. It's always the oatmeal raisin cookies that are left over on the cookie platters. *How did they earn a spot with chocolate chip and macadamia nut?)* We need the jealous love of our God to save us from the pathetic loves that give us a fleeting sense of confidence! Could we be rescued from these and turn back to our husband-God and his covenant love? Practically, could we turn away from perfectionism, the gym, the scale, and impressive homes and return to the true love of God? His love for us is enough because it is not based on our loveliness but on his faithfulness.

What do we learn about God in chapter 3? As we read that Hosea is buying Gomer back, we learn that God's love is scandalous. The wife's behavior has defamed her husband and has made her a captive, yet he rescues her. Her rejection of him is disgraceful and offensive, yet he seeks to restore the marriage, again.

Her behavior has left her at either a slave auction or a brothel. Either way, she is owned by someone and has a debt to pay.

From the outside, this is frustrating! How could this woman allow it to get this bad? How could she experience the forgiveness and salvation of this husband-God and then return again to a lesser lover?

Israel behaved in the same way. Although God had saved them from Egyptian slavery, they walked back into slavery by disobeying God's covenant. As we have read, near the end of Hosea's ministry, Israel was taken captive by Assyria.

Do we see the ways that we are freed women but walk right back into slavery, just like Israel? When we confess our sins and receive the salvation of God, death's chains fall off of our hearts and we are liberated. However, too often we choose to live like prisoners whose debts and jail sentences have been canceled yet decide to live life within their unlocked prison cells. What is this anomaly that lets us be free but prefer captivity? We have the freedom to leave, yet the jail cell appears safer and more controlled. And so that is where we remain, within an unlocked jail cell, living as a prisoner. Although we are freed wives, we behave like captives.

What does this actually look like in our lives? What threatens our freedom as Christian women? John 8:34 explains that "everyone who practices sin is a slave to sin." Our sin is what imprisons us. Hebrews 12:1 calls it the "sin which clings so closely." The New International Version describes it as "the sin that so easily entangles." These sins are the subtle chains that sneak onto our once freed ankles. The jail cell door is wide open, yet I can't run out because of the sneaky sins that cling to me.

How do we find freedom? How are we rescued from subtle slavery? I believe that with quick and regular repentance, we find liberation. Rather than waiting for a huge, emotion-packed moment of confession, we need to include it into our daily routines. If some of the applications of this study have fallen flat for you, I wonder if you are thinking on too big of a scale. To remain free from the slavery of sin, we must not look only for outright rebellion against God but subtle and seemingly insignificant offenses. We need to repent from chronic bad attitudes, daily habits of disrespect, or withholding grace from those we love. Through daily repentance, we are rescued from the sins that want to sit heavily on our ankles. Through daily repentance, we find a way to remain free.

Gomer's freedom is bought by Hosea, and it was at the price of a female slave (Exodus 21:32). Hosea emptied his pockets and paid fifteen shekels of silver. But that wasn't enough. Her debts were greater than what he had in cash, so he had to give more. So he added a homer and lethek of barley.

As Gomer watched her husband hand the barley over to the slave trader, did she recall the Old Testament law? As she was returned to Hosea, with the scent of another man still on her clothes, did the law of barley send chills down her spine?

While we don't know if Gomer knew the law given to God's people hundreds of years earlier, we know that the law for an adulteress woman was severe. As Numbers 5 explains, if unfaithfulness was even suspected in a wife, she was brought before a priest. Her husband, aroused to jealousy, would present her to the priest and offer a tenth of an ephah of barley. The barley was called the "grain offering of jealousy," meant to draw attention to her infidelity. The priest would then speak a curse over her, saying that if she was guilty of this sin, suffering would enter her body;

her abdomen would be swollen but her womb barren. The priest would take a handful of dust from the tabernacle floor and put it in some holy water. Then he would etch the curse into a stone and wash off the dust into the water. The accused woman would then drink the bitter water, as if drinking the curse.

If she was wrongly accused, then the curse would not come upon her. However, if her husband's jealousy was founded and she had given her love to another, then the bitter water would leave her cursed.

I must tell you that when I first read this scripture, I was overcome with emotion. As I saw the contrast of what the Old Testament commanded and what Gomer received, tears poured down my face. Even now, I am broken as I attempt to put into words what I see in this scripture.

I can picture myself standing before a priest, my head hanging from the weight of my guilt. In so many ways, my husband-God has found me in the bed of the world. He has found me giving myself to selfish ambition, using his gifts for my own advantages, and bowing to the idols of wealth, comfort, and people pleasing. I see myself standing there trembling as the curse is pronounced.

Unlike some of the women from Numbers, I am *not* wrongly accused. My husband-God is *not* wrongly jealous. My heart is split; my affections for God are weak and shared across many lovers.

I can hear the sound of the curse being etched into the stone. I can smell the dust as it's disrupted and mixed with the holy water. I watch as the tabernacle dust pollutes the holy water and understand more clearly that I am but dust—that my rebellion turns holy things bitter. I hear the words of the curse, and they turn my blood cold.

In that moment, I believe I have a brief minute of awareness. I see my offense for what it is and forgo the attempt to justify it. I see that I love many things and love pleasing many men. I see that I sneak away from my first love to flirt with many lesser loves: perfectionism, popularity, and control. So I hand the barley over and step toward the bitter water—the holy water now bitter due to my unfaithfulness.

But in the last moment, I am stopped.

Jesus, my better priest, steps between me and the bitter water. He faces the Lord and says that he will drink it instead. Moments before getting the curse that I most definitely deserve, he goes before the Lord and offers to take the curse for me. And he drinks it because he loves me. In this moment, his love appears near scandalous—taking a punishment for an offense he didn't commit for a woman who would never be true to him.

Now because of grace, our shame doesn't put us before a condemning priest. Because of the gospel, we have a much greater priest presenting us to the Lord. Our priest is Jesus, and he takes the cup of God's punishment so that we can come before God like a pure and innocent bride.

Today, we can approach the throne of grace with confidence. Hebrews 4:16 says, "Let us then with confidence draw near to the throne of grace, that we may receive mercy and find grace to help in time of need."

Gomer, who *wasn't* wrongly accused by her jealous husband, was not brought near to a priest ready to curse her. She was, instead, brought near to her husband-God in covenant love. Hosea brought barley on her behalf, like the husband in Numbers, which brought attention to her weak love. Yet unlike the offering in Numbers, Hosea's offering paid her debt and she was freed from the chains of her debtor.

Are we not in the same fortunate situation as Gomer? Time after time, do we not wander off, away from our husband-God and right back into slavery to sin? Not long after salvation, do we not return to our old vices? Although covenant love has been given to us, we are prone to behave like captives rather than wives.

Just like Gomer, our husband-God comes after us while we are still sinning. And our husband-God provides a payment to buy us back. The price is high. He had to give everything. Jesus's blood was the ransom—a payment to free us from our slavery to sin. His scandalous love draws him to the brothel of perverted love and makes a payment so sufficient that we are liberated.

Even more, we are then given an invitation to dwell with him many days. For the countless time, he invites us to purity and closeness with him. But he makes the expectation clear: we must cut off our relationships with other lovers to live in nearness to him. We must make the cut with our past lovers. We must cut them out of our life and live in the marriage covenant our husband-God has for us.

Similar to the process explained in Deuteronomy 21, it is good for us to embrace the process of living near to our husband-God. We need to embrace the fresh start that we would no longer behave like a slave but like a beloved wife. Like the slave-turned-wife, we should be broken, contrite, and humbled as we learn how to live in covenant love (Psalm 51:17).

Hosea foretold of Israel living without kings or rulers, without sacrifice or sacred stones and without ephods or household gods. This became a reality during their years in exile in Assyria. For hundreds of years, they lived without a king, in a land of exile, and without their temple. Isn't it sad how each of these wasn't bad in the beginning? The kings of Israel were meant to lead God's people, but when their hearts were weak and they made faithless decisions, Israel was led astray. When their religious practices and beliefs were woven in with the religion of their neighbors, it led them astray. And an ephod, meant to symbolize the presence of God, ended up becoming a god itself. The Israelites treated the ephod like a god itself, and were led astray.

How gracious is our husband-God to remove the very things that lead us astray? At times, God removes from our lives things that do not seem evil or compromising at first glance. But he knows our hearts and how easily our love can contaminate otherwise good things. Sometimes we need him to remove someone that we look up to so that we can look only to him. Sometimes we even need our religion taken away so that what remains is relationship with him.

One of the richest seasons in my life was when a full-time ministry job came to a quick and painful end, as I mentioned earlier. A few years later, with many days of healing under our belt, my husband and I now call that season our "grace makeover." God allowed our prideful hearts and the idol of people pleasing to be exposed. Through this season of discipline, I saw how many lovers I gave myself to in a given week, even within the walls of a church. Because of this, God took away my "sacrifices" and "pillars." He took away some aspects of my religion, and he allured me near to him and spoke to my broken heart. He spoke to me about what harm I am capable of, as if taking me back to the Valley of Achor.

What followed such gracious discipline was covenant nearness.

THE BLACK VELVET BEHIND THE GOSPEL

HOSEA 4–10

The remainder of the book of Hosea contains sections of Hosea's sermons to the people of Israel. We will read and study chapters 4–14 with a bird's-eye view. Most commentators agree that if you understand the first three chapters, then you understand the general message of the book in its entirety. If you understand the depths of the marriage analogy, then you can grasp the remainder of the book.[20] This week we will study chapters 4–10, which focus on Israel being found guilty and the consequence for that verdict. In our final session, we will study chapters 11–14, where we read about the redemption of Israel. When the guilt feels heavy or the punishment weighs you down, sit tight in the power of God's word, knowing that a beautiful story of redemption is ours because of Jesus.

DAY 1

Read chapters 4 and 5.

From Hosea 4:1 and 4:6, what is the charge against Israel?

Do you recall, from chapter 2, what the original translation of "to know" is?

In light of that original meaning, what do you think God means when he accuses them of having "no knowledge" (Hosea 4:1)?

In verse 2 Hosea lists the Ten Commandments that Israel has broken. Because of these acts of unfaithfulness, Hosea 4:19 warns, "A wind has wrapped them in its wings." Of what was Israel being warned?

Recall what happened to Israel in 722 BC. Look again at 2 Kings 17:6–15.

Although they were warned, Israel seemed to doubt that distance from God would actually lead them to be exiles in a land far from Canaan. In what ways could a lack of personal nearness to God lead you much further from him than you ever intended?

From 5:6, why do you think they are taking their flocks and herds when they go to seek the Lord?

From the following verses, what does the Lord say about the sacrifices of his people?

Isaiah 1:11

1 Samuel 15:22

What does the Lord desire instead of sacrifices?

Have you ever noticed that you bring sacrifices to God rather than obey what he is asking of you? Why do you think you do that?

Rewrite Hosea 5:13 in your own words.

Where did God's people turn for help? Did it work?

In what ways do we turn to other powerhouses for a fix or healing? Today, how could you apply this and turn to God for healing?

DAY 2

Read chapter 6.

In this sermon, Hosea is painting a future scene again. From verses 1 and 2, what awaits God's people if they return to the Lord in repentance?

Isaiah 30:26 also speaks of this future day. From this verse, who wounded Israel?

As Hosea points his readers to the future when Christ will reign fully, what does Hosea encourage Israel to do in verse 3?

Turn to Philippians 3:10 and 3:14. How are Paul's words similar to Hosea's words?

What emotions are evoked when you read Hosea 6:3, as you imagine the dawn, the showers, and the spring rains?

Consider Lamentations 3:22–23.

Focusing on God's faithfulness encourages us to press on toward the goal of Christlikeness. Is there a situation in your life that needs this encouragement right now?

In contrast to God's daily faithfulness, how is Israel's love described in verse 4?

Note the "therefore" in verse 5 and fill in the blanks below, using the ESV.

Because Israel's love is like a _____, God has _____ ___ them by the _____.

Use a dictionary to find the definition of *hewn*.

Rather than the prophets, how does God now speak to us and transform us, according to Hebrews 4:12?

What tool do you picture when you read the definition of *hewn*? What tool do you picture when you read the actions of the word of God from Hebrews? How are they different?

From Hosea 6:6, what does God desire?

Rewrite verse 6 in your own words.

Practically, in what ways could you bring God a relationship instead of religion?

A DEEPER LOOK

WOUNDED BY GOD

Lamentations 3:21–23 are well-known verses, seen all over mugs and Pinterest pages. Yet there is an even greater comfort in them if we dig a bit deeper and read those verses in context.

Read all of Lamentations 3. How would you summarize this chapter?

Who does the author say has wounded him?

From Hosea 6:1, recall who Hosea says has wounded Israel.

As you saw in the study, Israel was "hewn by the prophets" (Hosea 6:5). Recalling the definition of *hewn*, what tools would you use to hew something?

In contrast, Hebrews 4:12 explains that we are pierced by the word of God. What is the word capable of dividing?

1.

2.

3.

I am a nurse and currently work on a surgical oncology floor. One of our patient populations is cancer patients who have just undergone surgery to have cancer removed. I watch the surgeon round on their patients, and not once have I seen a patient point to his or her healing incisions and then at the surgeon and say, *"How dare you?* You did this to me! *How could you?"* Why not? Because they have just undergone that kind of tearing and wounding that has removed what would keep them from life. They have been wounded by the surgeon, but it served a purpose. The surgeon has struck them down so that he can bind them up. The surgeon used a scalpel, sharper than any ax or machete, so that he could go deep and close enough to discern between healthy cells and cancerous cells.

God's word does the same. The God-breathed words of the Bible are able to go in, with precision and exactness, and divide between what is good and healthy and what will kill and destroy. As Hebrews says, God's word cuts in deep and separates what in our life comes from belief and what comes from unbelief.

From this section of Hosea and Hebrews, I see a couple challenges for us to take on, as women, when we sense we are being wounded by God.

1. Rather than crumbling in self-pity, could we lean into our surgeon-God's goodness? Rather than causing a scene because life is hard and it seems we can't catch a break, could we accept this season of discipline and let God change us?

2. Could we allow ourselves to be trained by God's word? When our wounds ache or our incisions are slow to heal, could we lean into the word of God and let it go deep,

revealing what is under the surface that will hurt and destroy us? Could we study his word hard and let truth guide our days?

Here's the great comfort in this challenge: Jesus has been there. Jesus endured great hostility and great wounds (from God even!) so that we can come near to God and experience his love.

DAY 3

Read chapter 7.

When Hosea began his ministry in Israel, the country was prospering, which then led to them turning from God. However, near the end of his time, their political and financial situation became very unstable, just as Hosea had warned.

Recalling this context of Israel during Hosea's time, what is happening to their kings (verses 3 and 7)? Refer to 2 Kings 15:8–14.

Read 2 Kings 17:1–6. Which verse in Hosea 7 references this scripture?

Describe Israel's behavior as Hosea describes it in 7:14.

God says, through Hosea, that although Israel is emotional, it is not a brokenness that he honors. (I'll be the first to confess I'm quite good at causing a scene, throwing pity parties and channeling Eeyore like a pro but not always grieving over my sin.) Does grieving over difficulties and grieving over our sin produce difference emotions? Explain.

Consider 2 Corinthians 7:9–11. What does godly grief produce?

Recall a time that you had godly grief and describe it below.

Hosea also says that they "gash themselves" for grain and wine (Hosea 7:14). Read 1 Kings 18:20–39. What do the prophets of Baal do to themselves to evoke a response from Baal?

Recall from chapter 2, why do they not have grain and wine at this time?

Israel was trying to control God and evoke him to do as they wished. In what ways do we try to manipulate God to get what we want?

DAY 4

Read chapter 8.

Rewrite the ominous warning of 8:1 in your own words.

According to verse 2, what does Israel cry to God now that they are being disciplined?

Compare to Matthew 7:21–22. Why do you think this person says, "Lord," twice?

How are all of these people hoping they will convince God to hear and accept them?

Israel made an alliance with Assyria, and in this way, they sowed (planted) the wind. According to verse 7, what will they reap from this alliance?

Trusting in the gods of our neighbors is as ridiculous as trusting in the wind and can reap destruction as great as tornadoes. Recall the image of Gomer's alliance with weak lovers turning on her from Hosea 2:9–13.

Bravely recall the dark years of middle school with me. Perhaps you were like me (and every teen, romantic-comedy movie), and after finally working my way into the popular group, it was just days before they turned on me. (It's almost funny now, twenty years later.) In similar ways, have you ever experienced your friendships with the world turning on you?

What are the volatile and unstable things on which we depend?

From Hosea 9:1, what has Israel loved instead of her husband-God?

Where does she commit this unfaithfulness?

Threshing floors were where the harvested crops were gathered and manually separated. From what we have learned about Baal worship and what we saw in Gomer's experience, why do you think threshing floors became a place of Baal worship and harlotry?

Consider this: if Israel understood that God was the giver of life and provider of their needs, what might they have done at threshing floors rather than prostitute themselves?

According to verse 10, what happened at Baal-peor? Turn to Numbers 25:1–3 to read the context.

Hosea 9:10 says they "became detestable like the thing they loved." Read 2 Kings 17:15. How do we become what we worship?

DAY 5

Read chapter 10.

From verse 1, how did Israel respond when it was flourishing?

Why do you think it built more altars and pillars? (To whom was it giving credit for the political and agricultural success?)

What is your personal tendency when you are in a season of flourishing? Do you stray away from God or come nearer to him? Explain.

The majority of chapters 6–10 is so hard to read. They are heavy, as the punishment for an unrepentant heart is described thoroughly to Israel. Yet at the very end of this week's passage, we find a reminder of the everlasting covenant of our husband-God. Can you identify which verse speaks of hope?

Read 10:12 in both the NIV and the ESV.

What does Hosea tell Israel to sow (or plant) from this verse?

What will they then reap?

How does Galatians 6:8 further explain this verse?

Elliott's commentary sums this verse up beautifully. "This momentary rift in the storm cloud shows the light behind it."[21]

The light behind the darkness of chapters 6–10 is the hope of Jesus! By grace alone, we can study these difficult chapters, allow the weightiness to sit on our hearts, and still hope in the redemption of Jesus.

THE BLACK VELVET BEHIND THE GOSPEL

As Hosea traveled around the northern kingdom of Israel, preaching sermons to God's unfaithful bride, he drew from his very personal experience with Gomer. Chapters 4–10 were sermons of warning as well as accusations against unrepentant Israel.

On so many days, the words of Hosea behave like the room of mirrors at the carnival. Do you know what mirrors I am referring to? The unflattering mirrors that give you short, chubby legs and weird, wide faces. Hosea has placed us in front of these unflattering mirrors, as we have looked at the many angles of our unfaithfulness. Yet while this is a major theme of the book, God's word will not leave us condemned and rejected. When we behold the worst view of ourselves, we must believe that it will be repaired by the mercy of God, his faithfulness to a covenant, and the promise of Jesus. Let this hope encourage you as you continue in this study.

In chapter 4, Hosea tells the people of Israel that they are keeping God at a distance, just like Gomer kept him at a distance and filled in the space with other lovers. He tells them that they do not truly know God. He uses the word *yada*, which refers to a husband knowing his wife intimately. This teaches us that God doesn't want a mere head knowledge of him but an intimacy with his people. God wanted the Israelites to know him like a bride knows her husband, rather than how an employee knows his boss.

Hosea points out that the people of God have broken the law, as he lists out many of the Ten Commandments. He charges them with leaving God and instead cherishing whoredom and new wine, much like Gomer who left her husband, literally, to cherish another man's love (Hosea 4:10–11).

When we forsake a personal nearness with God, whatever we are clinging to instead will lead us much farther from our husband-God than we ever imagined. When we fill the bed of our hearts with many lovers, pushing our husband-God to the margins, we will soon find ourselves feeling quite impersonal with God. While we may not intend to be unfaithful, our entertaining of other lovers, or just flirting with the loves of this world, begins to crowd out the love we once had for God. And eventually we no longer have room for our husband-God in our hearts and are left with a mere head knowledge of him. The thought of him no longer stirs our affections or warms our hearts. Sadly, encountering his presence then leads to awkwardness rather than comfort.

The next accusation brought against Israel is that they have religion but not a relationship with God. Hosea warns the people that although they will bring their flocks and herds to seek God, they will not find him. Can you picture the Israelites scared of the threats of military giants breathing down their necks? So they begin sacrificing their herds, hoping God will be pleased with their offering and save them from Assyria?

Yet like a husband that has been betrayed, he doesn't want gifts from his unfaithful wife. Why not? Why wouldn't a new car or new golf clubs win back the favor of the betrayed husband? He wants the woman to understand the brokenness that her unfaithfulness has caused. He needs her to understand that her behavior has caused a fracture so severe that mere gifts won't mend it. The betrayed husband wants his wife, her repentant heart, and her love. He doesn't merely want her to acknowledge that she knows him; he wants her affections.

Similar to when Hosea brought Gomer home from her other lovers, Hosea didn't ask her to pay him back the silver and the barley. He invited her to dwell with him, to belong only to him. She was to take the time needed to no longer think like a slave but like a beloved wife. She was to remain near to him in faithful commitment and to break her ties with lesser lovers.

God is inviting us to bring him our heartfelt obedience rather than our sacrifices. He desires that we live a holy life, free from the contamination of the world's desires. Our lip service or the hours we give to our church don't cover up our unfaithfulness. Our good deeds or the money we sacrifice for the church building isn't primarily what our husband-God desires of us. He desires a broken and contrite heart that obeys out of love.

In chapter 6, we read a portion of one of Hosea's sermons where he speaks of the future day of Christ. Just like at the end of chapter 1, Hosea points to the end days when Christ will reign fully and sin will no longer affect this world. Hosea invites the Israelites to return to the Lord. Although they have been wounded and torn by God's discipline, Hosea tells his audience that God will not leave them wounded. He will heal them and bind up their wounds.

Like a doctor that surgically cuts someone open to remove a cancerous tumor and then precisely binds them back up, we too are torn by God to have our sin removed. No lesser intervention will be enough. A drastic means is necessary. Any remaining disease will spread and cause death.

With the hope of their wounds being healed, Hosea invites God's people to press on to know the Lord. He points his audience to God's faithfulness, to encourage belief in this God who wounds but also heals. He is as steady as the dawn, and his faithfulness is as refreshing as the spring rains.

When we sense that we are experiencing discipline, can we rely on our steady and faithful God enough to remain on the metaphorical operating table? Rather than rushing the process or jumping down to resume control, could we remain there and trust that healing will come? As he wounds us to remove every caustic inch of our hearts, can we believe that he will make us whole again? Can we trust his heart for us and his purpose for our life enough to tarry up on that table? Our husband-God's hand is strong and mighty and can feel heavy during times of discipline. Yet it is also delicate and meticulous, like a surgeon removing our hearts of stone and replacing them with hearts of flesh. He loves us too much to let the disease of sin hide within and spread.

So let us take Paul's words to heart when he states his goal to know Christ and to share in his sufferings (Philippians 3:10). May the goal of intimacy with Christ encourage us to press on to know him—to press on through seasons of discipline and through seasons of pain, or loss, or insult. Let us endure discipline well, knowing that its purpose is to defeat sin and repair our intimacy with our husband-God. Take comfort in the jealous love of our husband-God who has gone to extreme measures to bring us to him and will continue to work for our good. Lean into this process so that we may know him and his salvation.

Hosea hints at Jesus by saying, "After two days he will revive us; on the third day he will raise us up" (Hosea 6:2). While this may remind us of Christ, we must see the stark difference between our wounds and the death of Jesus. Where our sin and rebellious hearts invite the discipline of God, Jesus took the sufficient penalty of death. Jesus was rejected by God for three days so that we would never have to be.

In chapter 7, Hosea describes a very emotional Israel, as it finds itself between a rock and hard place. It has made alliances with Assyria but then sought Egypt's favor. Assyria has discovered its two timing and then besieged it. Israel is surrounded and scared. Hosea describes the people as wailing on their beds but still with their hearts far from God. They are feeling the emotion of impending doom yet still are not crying tears of repentance. In the ESV, Hosea says that they "gash themselves to get wine and grain" (Hosea 7:14). Once again mixing the practices of Baal worship and worship of the true God, they are behaving similarly to the prophets of Baal in 1

Kings 18. As was common for Baal worship, the worshippers would often mutilate their bodies, cut themselves, and even sacrifice their children to provoke Baal to answer on their behalf.

Have you ever noticed our modern-day attempts to manipulate God to get what we want? As women we may be tempted to skillfully use our emotions to prompt God to behave in a way that will change our circumstances. How often do we feel conviction of sin but don't let it draw us back to God? We can cause a pretty good scene when life gets difficult yet continue to behave like those who do not know God. We feel big emotions but don't let them draw us to a big cross.

Instead, we think that what we need are our "grain" and "wine." When life looks uncertain, we convince ourselves that our greatest need is more money, better health, and a firm plan—the aspects of life that make us feel safe. So we cry out to God for these things and draw lots of attention to our need. Yet how much more do we need our hearts to cry out for our gracious God to change us? More than the false securities of this world, we need new hearts from God. We need the grace to endure the tough seasons of discipline well so that we may experience the covenant nearness on the other side of them.

Hosea paints a doomsday image as he speaks to the Israelites in chapter 8. He tells Israel to prepare the military trumpets to blow, warning them of Assyria encircling Israel like a vulture. Lest the people begin to feel self-pity, he immediately explains why. "Because they have transgressed my covenant and rebelled against my law" (Hosea 8:1).

Israel's response to God at this time is to try to convince God that they are indeed close to him. They say, "My God, we—Israel—know you" (Hosea 8:2). Similar to those turned away from heaven in Matthew, they say, "Lord, Lord …" As if saying, "No, really, God, you and I are close." But because this husband-God knew their hearts, this late lip service would not suffice. The imposters at heaven's gates were trying to convince God that he should know them because of their great deeds of righteousness and their flashy faith. While they deceived many that they were spiritual giants, their hearts were far from him.

We must acknowledge that what our husband-God desires from us comes from the inside out. Rather than a relationship built primarily on what can be seen, our husband-God wants covenant behavior to flow from a heart that is true. When we experience his holiness and his pure love for us, it works its way out of our hearts and shows up in holy living.

What he desires first and foremost is our hearts. He desires a heart that loves him and beats for nearness to him. He desires a love that works its way out from our inner souls to our actions and passion for him that surfaces as obedience and thankfulness for his covenant love.

One of the richest seasons in my life came during a relatively quiet time. Sandwiched between seasons of ministry and productivity, I experienced rich intimacy with Christ. It was a period of healing, as God had recently removed the poisonous sin of pride and people pleasing. I was recovering from the soul surgery God had graciously performed on me, and I was preparing for what the next season would entail. There was no flashy faith in that year. There were no accolades from the masses. There was no high-profile work for God. I struggled with impatience and was tempted to rush the repair work of God. I struggled with doubt, thinking that if I didn't work for God, maybe he wouldn't bless me or love me. In that year, God drew me near as I healed (from my own sin and the sins of others) and as I learned to just quietly be faithful. He taught me that he wants me to love him with more authenticity and less show. He wanted to bring in more relationship and less religion. There has been no sweeter year in my life.

Have you experienced a difficult season in your life that led you to more intimacy with God? Have you experienced a season of loss or change that God has used to redefine your faith? Our husband-God's love is so extravagant that it packs purpose, healing, and new life into such seasons.

Hosea continues to accuse Israel and warn her of the consequences of her unfaithfulness. Again in chapter 9, he defines her infidelity. She has loved a prostitute's wages (Hosea 9:1).

He also specifies where she loved these wages—on the threshing floor. The threshing floor was the place the harvest was gathered. All that had been planted and reaped was brought here and sorted. The threshing floor was a place to see your hard work pay off. In good years, this was where you got what you deserved.

Because of that, they were also places of great celebration. Once the crops were gathered, the farmers would host big parties at the threshing floor. We see this in the story of Ruth. From Ruth 3:6–15, we see Boaz, the husband-to-be of Ruth, celebrating harvest at his threshing floor.

Yet in those years, when God's people should have been celebrating the provisions he had given them, they would worship Baal for their harvest. The threshing floors became like our bars filled with worship of sex and drink. Israel is accused of playing the harlot at these threshing floors.

Hosea explains to the people that the threshing floor and wine vat shall no longer feed them and that the new wine shall fail them (Hosea 9:2). Can we hear God say a similar truth to us? The threshing floor—the place where we believe that this world or our strength gives us all we need—will leave us unsatisfied and thirsty. We love giving ourselves to many weak loves, and we pat ourselves on the back for the great harvest we are reaping. So we raise a glass to the god of good work ethic, wise financial planning, or good health. In this moment, we believe we deserve a reward for our efforts.

Yet the place where we see our abundance and give our hearts to whoever will party with us will become a place of hunger and thirst. The fruit we reap in this scene is spoiled and will not feed us. The wine we drink at this orgy will fail us, leaving us parched. This behavior and wrong thinking will lead us to a land of exile from the land of the Lord.

Similar to Gomer's arrogance in her ability to make money through prostitution, Hosea accused Israel of becoming proud of its success. As Israel produced fruit and her status improved, they gave credit to Baal. In response to her success, the people added to their Baal worship by building more altars and pillars. Their punishment for this arrogance would be fear, grief, and shame.

What temptations do you face when you are in a season of success? When you are flourishing and seeing your goals come to fruition, do they draw you near to God or do they allure you away from him? We should take the words found in Deuteronomy 8:17–18 to heart, to be careful to take credit for the good things in our lives.

> Beware lest you say in your heart, "My power and the might of my hand have gotten me this wealth." You shall remember the Lord your God, for it is he who gives you power to get wealth, that he may confirm his covenant that he swore to your fathers, as it is to this day.

Ten chapters deep into a book heavy with accusations and punishments, a bit of hope is welcomed. This storm cloud, full of just accusations of Israel's unfaithfulness, splits open in chapter 10. Hosea tells his audience to plant righteousness rather than sin. He preaches that they should reap unfailing love rather than injustice. The result will be that they will be watered well with God's righteousness rather than eating the fruit of lies. He invites them to break up the hard ground of their hearts and cease trusting in their own ways or in their earthly confidences.

Pause for a moment and take comfort in this invitation. There is a beam of hope. There is a light breaking through the darkness. This book has been heavy at times (okay, most of the time), but please recall that our frail and capricious affections for God can serve as the black velvet behind the treasure of the gospel. Our husband-God's love contrasts greatly to our own. Like a diamond of unmerited love, God's love for us shines all the brighter against the darkness of our sin.

The invitation at the end of this fire and brimstone sermon is the gospel. Despite our hard hearts and trusting in our own way, we are invited to seek the Lord. Ezekiel 11:19 says that God can "remove the heart of stone from their flesh and give them a heart of flesh." When intimacy with our husband-God turns cold, our hearts begin to harden like an unplowed ground. Yet the Lord that has been wronged by his people is allowing them to seek him and to find him. And when they find him, they find righteousness and unfailing love. Let this redeeming love encourage you as you move into the last week of this study.

FREELY LOVED

HOSEA 11–14

DAY 1

Read chapter 11.

In this sermon by Hosea, he uses a new analogy. What different analogy does he use in chapter 11:1–4?

From verse 1, what memory does Hosea want to evoke in the Israelites?

Why do you think he does this?

Within chapter 11, Hosea recalls the many ways that God demonstrated his love to his people, from the beginning. How is God's love displayed to his children, according to the following verses?

Hosea 11:1

Hosea 11:3a

Hosea 11:3b

Hosea 11:4a

Hosea 11:4b

Let's look a little bit closer at each demonstration of faithful love. According to 1 Peter 2:9, what is Israel called away from? What is it called to?

What role does a parent play in a child learning to walk?

How does God title himself, in Exodus 15:26?

How did God lead young Israel away from Egypt? Read Exodus 13:21–22.

Read Exodus 16:4–7 to see how God bent down and fed them.

Of these five ways that Hosea explains God displays his love, which have you experienced recently?

DAY 2

Despite Israel's unfaithfulness to God, what gracious rhetorical question does God ask in Hosea 11:8a? Substitute your name for "Ephraim" (Israel's largest tribe) and "Israel" and write it out below.

Pause for a moment and let this truth take root in your heart: God's love will never leave you. No sin of the past or rebellion of the future will ever change his love for you. Read Deuteronomy 4:24–31 to understand how this can be true.

Specifically, how is God described in Deuteronomy 4:24 and 4:31?

From Hosea chapters 1–3, where did we see Hosea's mercy toward Gomer?

Throughout this study, we have seen God remain faithful to his covenant—faithful even when his people are faithless (2 Tim 2:13). Recall a time in your life that God was especially merciful to you.

Rewrite Hosea 11:10–11 in your own words.

What causes God's children to return to him in verse 10?

How does Proverbs 1:7 help us understand Hosea 11:10?

How could an appropriate understanding of the fear of the Lord lead you toward godliness? Consider Proverbs 31:30.

A DEEPER LOOK

THE WOMAN WHO FEARS THE LORD

Read Hosea 3:5. Describe *how* God's children will return to him and his goodness.

Read Hosea 11:10. What animal is used to describe the Lord, and how do his children respond to his roar?

In Exodus 20, when God descended on Mount Sinai to give the law to his people, it was a frightful sight. There were thunder, lightning, and a thick cloud; the entire mountain was surrounded by smoke. What was the people's response in Exodus 20:18?

Where did they stand?

What was Moses's response to them in verse 20?

What purpose was their fear supposed to serve?

Our family has a young Labrador retriever named Shaq. (Shaquille O'Neal was my tomboy phase hero.) Although he is cute, Shaq has always been at the bottom of the totem pole for me; all of my energy has to go to making sure my three young boys don't form an alliance against me. Therefore, I have not spent a lot of time training and disciplining him. Because of this, he does not fear me.

How do I know this? Because when I am out in the front yard and yell, "Come, Shaq!" he does not come. In fact, he runs away. However, when my husband (who has trained and disciplined him from the beginning) yells, "Come!" Shaq comes.

Shaq's behavior teaches me something about fearing God. Shaq shows that when we fear someone in a way that provokes respect and awe, we would never run away. However, when we don't truly fear someone in authority, we run around and do our own thing. John Piper explains this phenomenon when he says, "If you are running from God because you are afraid of him, then you are not yet as afraid as you ought to be. In fact, your very flight is a mockery of God …"[22] When we are running from God or keeping him at a distance, then we have yet to understand what it means to fear him. When we stand far off, like the Israelites did at Mount Sinai, we still have much to learn about our God. When we accurately fear him, holding him in respect and awe, we will do three things.

1. We will remain close to him and come to him when he calls.

2. We will find victory over our sin. As Moses said to the children of God at the base of Mount Sinai, "That the fear of him may be before you, that you may not sin" (Exodus 20:20). We will not be perfect, but through this fear, we will find it easier to turn away from sin.

3. We will not fear. When we fear God, our other fears die away. When our eyes are fixed on the might and power of God, we no longer fear criticism, loss, or failure. When we understand that we are loved by the God who holds all the power in his hands, we realize that man can do nothing to us.

Are you running from God or keeping him at a distance? If so, could it be that you don't fear him?

Are you finding your affinity for a certain sin to be stronger than your ability to turn from it? If so, how could beholding the power and holiness of God help you?

Do you live with fear of man? Do you struggle with fear of criticism or failure? In what ways could drawing near to God and learning to fear him remove these fears?

DAY 3

Chapter 12

Read chapter 12.

In verse 1, who does Ephraim chase?

What do you think Israel wanted from Assyria and Egypt?

What do we want to obtain from our seemingly big, strong, and impressive "neighbors"?

Have you ever felt frustrated and exhausted from chasing them, like chasing the wind?

What individual does Hosea begin talking about in verse 2b?

Match the following to get the context on this founder of Israel:

Genesis 25:26   During birth, he grabbed the heel of his twin.

Genesis 25:29–34   Jacob dressed like his older brother, thus stealing the blessing of their father.

Genesis 32:22–32   Jacob wrestled with the angel of God through the night to obtain a blessing.

Genesis 35:9–15   Jacob manipulated his older brother, trading a pot of red stew for his brother's birthright.

Genesis 27:1–29   Jacob, changed by his encounter with the angel, met God at Bethel and received his promises.

Why do you think God wants Israel to think of Jacob at this time?

Recalling the whole study, how has the nation of Israel attempted to deceive God? Where has it taken control instead of trusting God?

In what ways do we do the same? Where in your life are you tempted to take control instead of trusting God?

In what ways has this book of the Bible made you wrestle with who God is?

In what ways has this book of the Bible made you wrestle with who you are?

DAY 4

Read chapter 13.

Verses 1–3 describe Israel's past, present, and future. Recall that in the early years of Hosea's ministry, Israel was strong politically and financially.

What did that season lead to, from verses 1 and 2?

There's a *therefore* in verse 3. Using verse 2, fill in the blanks to describe the consequences of Israel's idol worship.

Because Israel made _____ and kissed _____, they will be like the _____, _____, or _____.

Has sin in your life ever brought a death or quick end to something?

Rewrite verse 6 in your own words.

With what did Israel fill up?

With what did Gomer fill up (Hosea 2:5)?

Often in my life, I do not trust in the promises of God and, therefore, fill up on the empty promises of the world. So I fill up on what I think will satisfy me: success, financial stability, and the approval of man. Yet in John 10:10, Jesus says, "I came that they may have life and have it abundantly."

It is tempting to fill up on these blessings from God rather than respond in humble gratitude. Yet gratitude creates in us a sharp memory of God rather than forgetfulness as Israel displayed. Pause for a moment and spend time confessing to the Lord what ruins your appetite for him. What do you "graze" on that fills you up, dulling your hunger for God?

DAY 5

Read chapter 14.

Chapter 14 begins with the repentance of Israel. What does Hosea instruct the people to say to God?

What must they confess, from verse 3?

Look up the definition of *apostasy* (from verse 4 in the ESV). Write it out below.

From verses 4–7, what do we receive from God, after repentance?

Where will Israel dwell after it returns, according to verse 7?

Write out the comforting words of Psalm 91:1.

Recalling the entire study, what verse encouraged you the most?

How has your understanding of God as husband changed?

In what ways have you started to love God as husband, rather than serve him dutifully as a master?[23]

In what sections of this book did you most see grace make the way for a relationship with a holy God?

FREELY LOVED

Our final week begins with a comforting image, as God is portrayed as father and we as his beloved children. Briefly leaving the marriage analogy, God now gives Hosea the words to describe our relationship with God in a new and refreshing way. Like a young child finds comfort and assurance in the nearness of his or her parents, we can find great comfort in this analogy.

In chapter 11, Hosea takes Israel back to her days of youth, when God called her out of Egypt. Just like in 2:15, he brings to her mind's eye images of salvation and deliverance. Yet like a stubborn toddler, the more God called her, the more she resisted him and moved toward Baal. The more the father-God called Israel to himself, the more she ran off to the gods who couldn't see or hear her.

Hosea's words touch on the many ways that God displays his love to his children. In years heavy with accusation, Hosea's words likely brought life to the children of Israel. As we have been entrenched in heavy messages of warning, with themes like jealousy and sin, looking closely at some ways God displays his love will hopefully encourage you as we near the end of this study.

God calls those he loves. He calls them to hope, and he calls them out of darkness and into light. First Peter 2:9 describes Israel. "But you are a chosen race, a royal priesthood, a holy nation, a people for his own possession, that you may proclaim the excellencies of him who called you out of darkness into his marvelous light."

He says that he taught Ephraim (a name for Israel) how to walk. What a powerful image of a parent taking up a child after a stumble, pulling that child up by the arms. In the years following the Exodus, God taught the Israelites how to walk as his children, even when their faith faltered. Like a toddler who falls again and again and needs her parents to grab her by the arms and try yet again, Israel is upheld by their father-God.

Do you recall Hosea teaching Gomer how to live with him in chapter 3? After Hosea bought Gomer back from slavery, he taught her how to live with him, how to walk with him. He instructed her how to live like his wife rather than like a slave.

Where his children's sin led to injury—emotional, mental, or spiritual—God displayed his love by healing them, as he said in chapter 6. Although he allowed them to experience the consequences of rebellion, he mercifully healed them.

Hosea says that God leads his children with cords of kindness and bands of love (Hosea 11:4). He briefly uses the metaphor of animals, with a picture of a farm animal being carefully led by its owner. Recall how God led Israel by blocking her paths in chapter 2 and how he led and allured her out into the wilderness. It was his kindness that led her to repentance like bands of love.

Furthermore, he displays his love by easing or lightening her yoke. He explains that they are like animals that have had the heavy yoke removed from their back, as God had removed the yoke of Egyptian slavery from his children. Like Israel was freed from Egyptian slavery and Gomer freed from the chains of her debtor, Israel would be freed from the punishment its rebellion deserved.

We too are dearly loved children. By grace, we are called to Christ. We are called out of darkness and invited by name to live in the light. Once we are his, God teaches us how to walk in his ways and provides the wisdom to navigate life in a way that pleases him. When we stumble in our sin, he graciously lifts us up. He stabilizes our posture, sets our feet in the right direction, and helps us walk. How gracious is our father-God to teach us how to walk as his children! Time after time, when we get tripped up by our own sin, he picks us up by our arms, giving us another opportunity to reset. He does not leave us sitting on our backsides, feeling discouraged or disheartened. Furthermore, he doesn't leave us to figure it out by ourselves, independently from him. He wants to come near and help us as we learn to walk in a way that honors him in covenant love.

When in Christ, we too have the yokes of slavery removed from our shoulders. We no longer carry the heavy burden of the law because of the new covenant and grace. Where our sins place heavy yokes on us, our jealous husband-God puts us in Christ. We are freed from that weight and are given rest. In Matthew 11:28–30, Jesus said,

Come to me, all who labor and are heavy laden, and I will give you rest. Take my yoke upon you, and learn from me, for I am gentle and lowly in heart, and you will find rest for your souls. For my yoke is easy, and my burden is light.

Freed and lightened up in God's love, we are now led with cords of kindness. He does not lead us like a harsh master, with whips and burdensome yokes, but with bands of love. These bands lead us away from the doorsteps of weak lovers, away from the altars of false gods, and near to him.

God's love is so great for us that he bends down and feeds us. Just as God bent down and fed the Israelites with both manna and quail, he feeds us. Take a moment to assess the ways in which God is displaying his love for you today. Do you sense him calling you near to him and away from the chains of your Egypt? In what ways do you struggle to stay on your feet spiritually? What a grace that allows a holy God to come near to us, with an opportunity to begin again, each day. In what ways have you seen God push the reset button for you, forgetting your stumbles of yesterday and helping you start again today?

The many displays of God's love are clearly laid out in Hosea 11. When we recall these manifestations of his love, our invitation is simple: to accept his love. Yet although it sounds so simple, I think we often resist it.

I recall when I was in the throes of puberty, my dad came behind me and placed his hands on my shoulders to give me a back massage. Because I was a mess of hormones and insecurity, I immediately tensed my shoulders, resisting his attempt to love me. It's such a seemingly insignificant memory to recall so clearly, but I remember with clarity my dad saying, "Bekah, why did you tense up like that?" I mumbled something of no substance under my breath and went off (probably to attempt to straighten my frizzy, orange hair again), escaping from his attempt to love me.

God has brought this memory to my mind at several points during this study. Is this not what we do in response to God's displays of love? Rather than accepting the many ways he communicates love to us, in our stubbornness and insecurity, we resist him. We stiff-arm him and keep him at a safe distance. We believe that if he is an arm's length away, then he can't see how messed up and unlovable we truly are.

The invitation from God throughout the book of Hosea is to come close to him and allow him to love us like a husband. Where sin and shame tell us to keep him at a safe distance, grace allows and creates nearness. The plea from God, through Hosea, is to live in covenant love.

In chapter 12, God takes his people to the memory of one of their founding fathers: Jacob. After indicting Israel for multiplying falsehood, he begins to show the people that they are much like Jacob.

Jacob's story is found in Genesis. It begins with Jacob grabbing his older brother's heel during delivery. This act earned him a name that means "heel grabber" and "deceiver." Young Jacob lived up to his name. From birth he was sneaky, deceptive, and manipulative. As we read, he manipulated his brother for his birthright and then deceived his father for his blessing.

But then, forced to run away in fear of his brother, Jacob enters a season of discipline characterized by interpersonal conflict, hopes deferred, and some lingering bad habits of deception.

Jacob then has a night with God. As Hosea 12:3 explains, "In his manhood he strove with God." He wrestles with God. God takes him on, and Jacob holds his own. Could this be the jealous love of Israel's God that goes near to his people to obtain their hearts and their trust? Rather than writing him off, God came near to Jacob and allowed him to experience him in a way that would change him.

As dawn is breaking, Jacob courageously asks God for a blessing. Unlike the first blessing that he stole through manipulation, Jacob has now striven, wept, and sought God's favor.

God, who has graciously exhausted Jacob physically, now goes after his heart. God asks Jacob for his name. "Jacob," he makes him say out loud. "My name is Jacob; my name is Deceiver."

Did the duel pause for a moment, as Jacob instantly relived his failures of the past twenty years? His habit, like the country he was founding, was to be untrue. He had deceived his brother, his father, and his father-in-law.

Why did God see it good to bring up Jacob's weakness then? Had he not endured through the night with God? Had it not been a long enough night? Dawn was finally breaking, yet did it seem that God wanted to depress him by bringing up Jacob's regrets?

As we near the end of this study, are we growing tired of hearing how chronic our rebellion is? Are we weary of recalling our habits to deceive both God and man? Are we fatigued of assessing our often hard hearts?

There is great hope for us! The soul's relief, as it was for Jacob, is that we get to hear the healing words of the gospel. As if subtly revealing the gospel in one Old Testament sentence, God says to Jacob, "Your name shall no longer be called Jacob, but Israel, for you have striven with God and have prevailed" (Genesis 32:28).

It is like saying,

> You will no longer be Deceiver, Jacob. You are to be done with deceit. You now know what you are capable of. But now you will be known as Israel. You wrestled with me; you endured the night of discipline with me. You are bound to me, beloved. You have clung to me through this night, and I have sustained you. Dawn is breaking. Be new.

Through Hosea's words, God says to Israel,

> You are to be done with deception. You are to be done with your attempts to deceive me or manipulate me. You are capable of much harm, but I have called you to be my people. So hold fast to love and justice and wait continually for me. Cling to me, through the night and through discipline, and I will sustain you.

Our invitation is the same. God comes to us regardless of our past, our offenses, and our bad habits. But it will require wrestling with who we are and with who God is. When God graciously brings up our unfaithfulness, it is good for us to cling to him, rather than try to squirm out of his grip. In the moment following self-awareness, when despair or depression wants to move in, our husband-God speaks up first. He talks of new life, he talks of a new identity, and he talks of his jealous love for us. He reminds us that his story is one of redemption and fresh starts.

It is then that he embraces us, well before we prove ourselves to him. Long before we display trustworthiness or purity, he blesses us with his love and his nearness. What an amazing grace!

In chapter 13, we again hear Hosea accuse Israel of idolatry. A comfortable satisfaction led to pride, which led her to forget her husband-God. With hearts and bellies full, the God who saved her from Egypt has been forgotten and replaced with Baal. Israel has made statues of calves and is kissing them, giving its love to a lifeless statue.

Just as Gomer's desire for grain, wine, and flax had led her to her lovers, Israel's success has led her to Baal. But God's jealous love will not tolerate this competition. She is breaking the covenant that he gave her, and the consequences must be carried out. She will disappear like the morning mist. Her glory will fade away like the dew. Her success and very life will fly away like the chaff from the threshing floor. There is no salvation to be found in Baal; the Lord her God is her savior who has known her since the beginning, since she left Egypt.

I wonder if we could see how far our idol worship has come. Do we do more than desire the gods of our neighbors? Do we kiss them, in a way? Have our hearts wandered so far from our husband-God that we are now intimately involved with our lesser lovers?

Do we not receive blessings from our God, but instead of them drawing us toward him, do they lead us away? Rather than creating more of a hunger for God, we let them satisfy us. We become comfortable with our planned-out weeks, our like-minded friends, and our careers and settle into a dangerous satisfaction. That satisfaction leads to pride, and we begin to forget all that our husband-God has given us.

We must pray for wisdom during times of abundance. Having money, lots of friends, or success at work isn't bad in itself. However, knowing that our hearts are quick to wander, we should be attentive to the ways that we are like Israel. If you are in a season of financial stability, is your heart becoming full? Are you at risk of forgetting your husband-God? If you are in a season where you are loved—nobody says a bad thing about you—could you be at risk for thinking that your needs are met by the love of your friends? God's love is so jealous that it will redeem us from the chains of complacency.

The last chapter begins with an invitation that should surprise us. "Return, O Israel, to the Lord your God" (Hosea 14:1). We should be astonished that grace allows us to hear such an invitation. How gracious is our husband-God that there is still a way for us to return to him! So let's hasten to him, turn our backs on the false gods, and return to our God. What a merciful and patient husband-God who accepts our confession-filled apologies. What a faithful God who responds, unlike man, and keeps his covenant with his bride.

So let us ask him to take away our iniquity, to remove from our hearts all offenses to his holiness. Let's trust in his love enough to allow him to do the invasive heart work of sanctification. After months of seeing unflattering views of ourselves, the plea to return to the husband-God we have cheated on should still surprise our hearts. What an amazing grace that paves the way home for us!

Let's say to our savior, "Assyria will not save us" (Hosea 14:3). Our strength, our good reputations, and our self-effort will not save us. Our health, our homes, and our goodness do not provide us with our needs. "We will say no more, 'Our god', to the work of our hands" (Hosea 14:3). We will no longer make room in our hearts for the worship of false securities—not even our marriages, our kids, or our plan for life.

Not only do we have the option to return to God, but our repentance leads to healing. Although times of discipline may be necessary to rescue and redeem our hearts, God will pour out mercy, as he turns his anger from us. He will heal our apostasy and our waywardness, redeeming what was lost in our hearts. And he will love us freely!

We are not Hosea in this story, helping God call all the estranged women to himself. We are the sister of Gomer, and we are on the stand in the courtroom with a long list of accusations against us. We have been found guilty of much deceit and much unfaithfulness. But that is not our final sentence.

As Hosea's words have fallen accurately on our hearts, grace has saved us from the death sentence that we deserve. We are the woman doused in the mercy of God, the woman guilty but accepted, and the woman freed from our chains by Jesus.

Because of Jesus, the penalty we deserve passes over us. Instead of death, we get the healing blood of Jesus. Where our waywardness would leave us as orphans starved for mercy, the blood of Jesus allows us to return and rest beneath God's shadow. Because of the gospel packed within the writing of this Old Testament prophet, we receive the invitation to dwell in the shelter of the Most High and abide in the shadow of the Almighty (Psalm 91:1).

Because of the big picture story of the Bible, we get to be the rescued bride of God Almighty. So let's love him warmly, like a husband.

NOTES

INTRODUCTION

1. Jen Wilkin, author and speaker, is setting a new pace among women's ministry as she challenges women to become biblically literate by loving the Lord with their minds. She says, "The heart cannot love what the mind does not know." Her influence in my life, my study of the Word, and my writing is greatly appreciated. Wilkin, J. *Women of the Word: How to Study the Bible with Both Our Hearts and Our Minds*. Wheaton, IL: Crossway, 2014.

CHAPTER 1: THE GIFT OF A HUSBAND-GOD

2. Piper, J. "Call Me Husband, Not Baal." December 26, 1982. Retrieved July 5, 2016, from http://www.desiringgod.org/messages/call-me-husband-not-baal.

3. Smith, G.V. *Hosea, Amos, Micah: The NIV Application Commentary from Biblical Text to Contemporary Life*. Grand Rapids, MI: Zondervan Pub. House, 2001, 46.

4. There are many different thoughts on whether Gomer was a prostitute before marrying Hosea or if she was only unfaithful after her marriage. Smith, G.V. *Hosea, Amos, Micah: The NIV Application Commentary from Biblical Text to Contemporary Life*. Grand Rapids, MI: Zondervan Pub. House, 2001, 45.

5. Piper, J. "Call Me Husband, Not Baal." December 26, 1982. Retrieved July 5, 2016, from http://www.desiringgod.org/messages/call-me-husband-not-baal.

6. Wilkin, J. (2014). *Women of the Word: How to Study the Bible with Both Our Hearts and Our Minds*. Wheaton, IL: Crossway, 27.

7. MacArthur, J. (2005). *The MacArthur Bible Commentary: Unleashing God's Truth, One Verse at a Time*. Nashville, TN: Thomas Nelson, Inc., 971.

8. Piper, J. "Call Me Husband, Not Baal." December 26, 1982. Retrieved July 5, 2016, from http://www.desiringgod.org/messages/call-me-husband-not-baal.

CHAPTER 2: BROTHELS OF THE HEART

9. Smith, G.V. *Hosea, Amos, Micah: The NIV Application Commentary from Biblical Text to Contemporary Life.* Grand Rapids, MI: Zondervan Pub. House, 2001, 60.

10. Keller, T. *The Prodigal God: Recovering the Heart of the Christian Faith.* New York: Dutton, 2008.

11. Keller, T. *The Prodigal God: Recovering the Heart of the Christian Faith.* New York: Dutton, 2008, 41.

12. Calvin, Jean. English translation of book 1, chapter 11, section 8 of *Institution de la Religion Chrestienne*, 1560.

13. Kraft, A. *Good News for Those Trying Harder.* Colorado Springs, CO: David C. Cook, 2008, 189.

CHAPTER 3: A DOOR OF HOPE

14. Keller, T. *The Prodigal God: Recovering the Heart of the Christian Faith.* New York: Dutton, 2008, 42.

15. Smith explains the bride price in this way: "Thus, God himself gives his gifts of righteousness, justice, love, compassion, and faithfulness to cement this relationship into an unbreakable union that will last forever." Smith, G.V. *Hosea, Amos, Micah: The NIV Application Commentary from Biblical Text to Contemporary Life.* Grand Rapids, MI: Zondervan Pub. House, 2001, 63.

16. Hosea paints this millennial scene often. MacArthur, John. *The MacArthur Bible Commentary: Unleashing God's Truth, One Verse at a Time.* Nashville, TN: Thomas Nelson, 2005, 973.

17. Piper, J. "Call Me Husband, Not Baal." December 26, 1982. Retrieved July 5, 2016, from http://www.desiringgod.org/messages/call-me-husband-not-baal.

18. Keller, T. *The Prodigal God: Recovering the Heart of the Christian Faith.* New York: Dutton, 2008, 74.

CHAPTER 4: INVITED NEAR

19. Piper, J. "Call Me Husband, Not Baal." December 26, 1982. Retrieved July 5, 2016, from http://www.desiringgod.org/messages/call-me-husband-not-baal.

20. *Hosea 10 Commentary: Ellicott's Commentary for English Readers,* 1905. Retrieved August 2, 2016, from http://www.studylight.org/commentaries/ebc/hosea-10.html.

CHAPTER 6

21. Piper, J. "A Woman Who Fears the Lord Is to Be Praised." Retrieved October 22, 2016, from http://www.desiringgod.org/messages/a-woman-who-fears-the-lord-is-to-be-praised.

22. Piper, J. "Call Me Husband, Not Baal." December 26, 1982. Retrieved July 5, 2016, from http://www.desiringgod.org/messages/call-me-husband-not-baal.

SMALL GROUP QUESTIONS

WEEK 1

1. Have you studied the book of Hosea before? If so, how would you summarize the book?

2. Define the metaphor used in this book. Who does Hosea symbolize? Who does Gomer symbolize? In what ways do you think of God as your husband? Does this concept comfort you or make you uncomfortable? Why?

3. What were the names of Gomer's children? What did you learn by looking at the meaning of these names?

4. Much like the king at the battle of Jezreel, when I behave like I am god, I hurt a lot of people and leave a mess in my path. Have you ever noticed that when you make yourself a god you create a disaster? Explain.

5. Do you more naturally see yourself as Hosea or Gomer? Explain.

6. What did you learn about God in this first week of study? What was the good news in week 1?

WEEK 2

1. What is Ezekiel 16 about? From Ezekiel 16:59–63, what is the good news for the Lord's faithless bride?

2. In Hosea 2, we learned that Gomer was confused about who gave her what she needed and wanted for "the good life." How did this misunderstanding hurt her marriage?

3. What was the first rescue mission of God (from day 4)? Have you ever sensed that God has blocked a path that would lead you away from him? Have you ever seen God slow you from your runaway path from him? Explain.

4. Why did we read Luke 15:11–24? What similarities do you see in this story and Hosea 2?

5. What was the second rescue mission of God (from day 5)? Have you ever felt exposed? Has there been a situation that left you with your sin, mistakes, and imperfections on display for all to see?

6. What did you learn about God in week 2? What did you learn about yourself?

WEEK 3

1. What is God's third rescue mission (from day 1)? Can a season in the desert be a good experience? Explain.

2. From Hosea 2:15, what two things does God do for his bride in the wilderness?

3. What change do we see in how Gomer answers her husband in Hosea 2:15–16? Why is this important?

4. Why did we return to Luke 15? In what ways did the older son seem to view his prodigal dad as master? In what ways do you view God as master rather than husband?

5. Hosea 2:20 says, "And you shall know the Lord." The original translation of "to know" is the Hebrew word *yada*, which refers to a husband knowing his wife intimately. How would your relationship with God look differently if you knew him with a *yada* knowing rather than merely a head knowledge?

6. What did you learn about God in week 3? What good news was there in week 3?

WEEK 4

1. From chapter 3, what has Gomer done again? What is she loving instead of God?

2. Raisins are also an aphrodisiac meant to arouse desire. Much like Israel, we can turn to what makes us feel love or feel loveable. What do you turn to so that you can feel love? What do you turn to so that you can feel lovely? What effect does this have on your relationship with God?

3. Gomer has made herself a slave, behaving like a captive rather than a wife. Are there ways that we do this? Consider John 8:34.

4. The word for *covenant* comes from a Hebrew root *karath*, which means "to cut." From what does the Gomer have to make a cut? What needs to be removed or cut from your life so that you may live in nearness to God?

5. Gomer was a freed woman who returned to slavery. Do we see the ways that we are freed women but walk right back into slavery, just like Israel and Gomer? What threatens our freedom as Christian women? Consider John 8:34 and Hebrews 12:1.

6. What did you learn about God in week 4? What good news stood out to you this week?

WEEK 5

1. Do you recall, from chapter 2, what the original of that original meaning, what do you think God means when he accuses them of having "no knowledge" (Hosea 4:1)?

2. Although they were warned, Israel seemed to doubt that distance from God would actually lead them to be exiles in a land far from Canaan. In what ways could a lack of personal nearness to God lead you much farther from him than you ever intended? How would viewing God as husband-God prevent this?

3. Hosea 6:3 says, "Let us know, let us press on the know the Lord; his going out is as sure as the dawn; he will come to us as the showers, as the spring rains that water the earth." Focusing on God's faithfulness encourages us to press on toward the goal of Christlikeness. Is there a situation in your life that needs this encouragement right now?

4. God says, through Hosea, that although Israel is emotional, it is not a brokenness that he honors. Does grieving over difficulties and grieving over our sin produce difference emotions? What does godly grief produce? Consider 2 Corinthians 7:9–11.

5. Threshing floors were where the harvested crops were gathered and manually separated. From what we have learned about Baal worship and what we saw in Gomer's experience, why do you think threshing floors became a place of Baal worship and harlotry (Hosea 9:1)?

If Israel understood that God was the giver of life and provider of their needs, what might they have done at threshing floors rather than prostitute themselves?

6. What did you learn about God in week 5? What good news did you find in these scriptures?

WEEK 6

1. What causes God's children to return to him in Hosea 11:10? How does Proverbs 1:7 help us understand this? How could an appropriate understanding of the fear of the Lord lead you toward godliness?

2. In Hosea 12, we read about Jacob. Recall what you learned about him and how it related to the country of Israel.

3. In what ways has this book of the Bible made you wrestle with who God is? In what ways has this book of the Bible made you wrestle with who you are?

4. Read Hosea 13:5–6. It is tempting to fill up on these blessings from God rather than respond in humble gratitude. Yet gratitude creates in us a sharp memory of God rather than forgetfulness as Israel displayed. Spend time confessing to the Lord what ruins your appetite for him. What do you "graze" on that fills you up, dulling your hunger for God?

5. What did you learn about God in the last week of study? What good news did you read in this final week?

6. In what ways has loving God like a husband changed your heart and mind? In what ways has it changed your behavior?